Historic Garmisch Promenade Coloring Book

A brief tour of the vibrant, open-air, art gallery that is the Lüftlmalerei of Garmisch-Partenkirchen in Bavaria, Germany

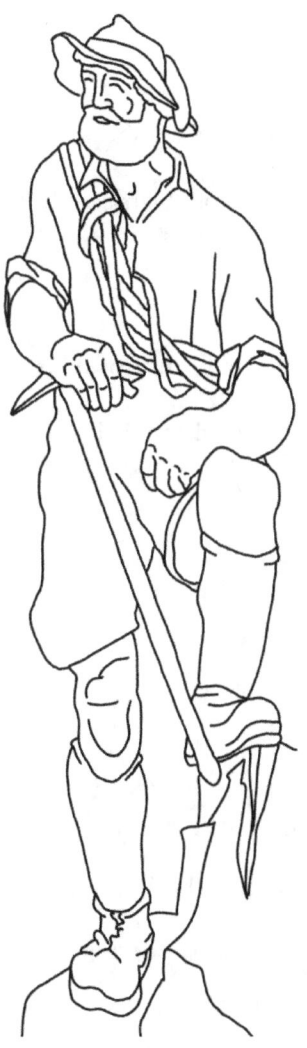

Justin Vazquez

For my brother, Jesse,

a painter and an artist, himself;
I am always proud to be your player two,
through this adventure, and every other.

With special thanks to Jake Doherty,

whose passion for All Things Garmisch helped inspire this book,
and whose breadth of history and ability to spin a yarn I can only hope to one day match;

and Josef Ostler, town historian,

who was nothing but charming in afternoon phone calls
sharing his incredible knowledge of these paintings with me.

Additional copies of this book in either English or German are available at both Amazon.com and Amazon.de

INTRODUCTION

When you think of Southern Germany, you likely picture Lederhosen, Oktoberfest, or King Ludwig's fairytale castle. But just as quintessentially Bavarian are the murals on the sides of homes, businesses, and even barns – scenes from the Bible, the lives of Saints, or just rustic, rural life.

In the town of Garmisch-Partenkirchen these outdoor wall paintings are called *Lüftlmalerei*. In German, *Luft* means "air," and *Malerei* means "painting;" so the name "Lüftlmalerei" means an "airy" outdoor "painting."

This style of art can be traced back two thousand years, to the 1st century, when Romans decorated the walls of their estates with plaster and stucco. Dye and pigments were painted into wet plaster and, once it dried, there was a waterproof and lasting *fresco* (Italian for "fresh") painting.

As Christianity spread from Rome north beyond the Alps, a cult of saints began to form. As their cults grew, saints' remains became relics – magical objects believed to be capable of performing miracles long after the saint had died. Saints' graves became places people would make special trips to see. Artists used the plaster fresco technique to paint the walls of pilgrimage churches to tell the stories of the lives of saints.

While the style first spread as church decoration, it was quickly copied. Soon, throughout Germany, town halls, market stalls, and city walls were painted with images of important events, major battles, and stories from the lives of kings. Gate towers were covered with impressive pictures of fearsome warriors carrying the city's coat of arms on their shields. German legends were writ large across imposing castle walls. It wasn't long before well-to-do Germans began decorating their homes in the same way – just like the Romans had, a millennium before.

By the 18th century, as fresco painting was falling out of fashion in the major cities, it began to take hold in the foothills of the Alps. Traders, warehouse owners, and craftsmen started to display their wealth on the walls of their own homes. Religious motifs were still popular, but so were references to local, everyday life. Those who could afford to, could have their patron saint, family crest, or some simple slogans extolling the wisdom of rural life tattooed on the stucco walls of their simple *Hof* ("estate").

Alpine homes are perfect for this style of painting. The walls of Bavarian and Tyrolean farmhouses are almost always plastered white, providing an ample canvas for fresco painters to fill with bright, cheerful colors.

The pedestrian zone in Garmisch – which stretches along Marienplatz, Mohrenplatz, and Am Kurpark street – has been a hub of commercial activity for hundreds of years. In all that time, the shops and buildings have been covered with Lüftlmalerei. If you walk down the street today, you might wonder, what do these particular paintings mean? Why are they here and what do they show?

This picture book, like a walk down that promenade, tells some of the stories of Garmisch-Partenkirchen, its people, and its place in history – a story written in its Lüftlmalerei.

As you put your own creative talents to work coloring these images, you can see what these paintings actually look like and learn about the artists who painted them by going online to https://lueftlmalerei.com.

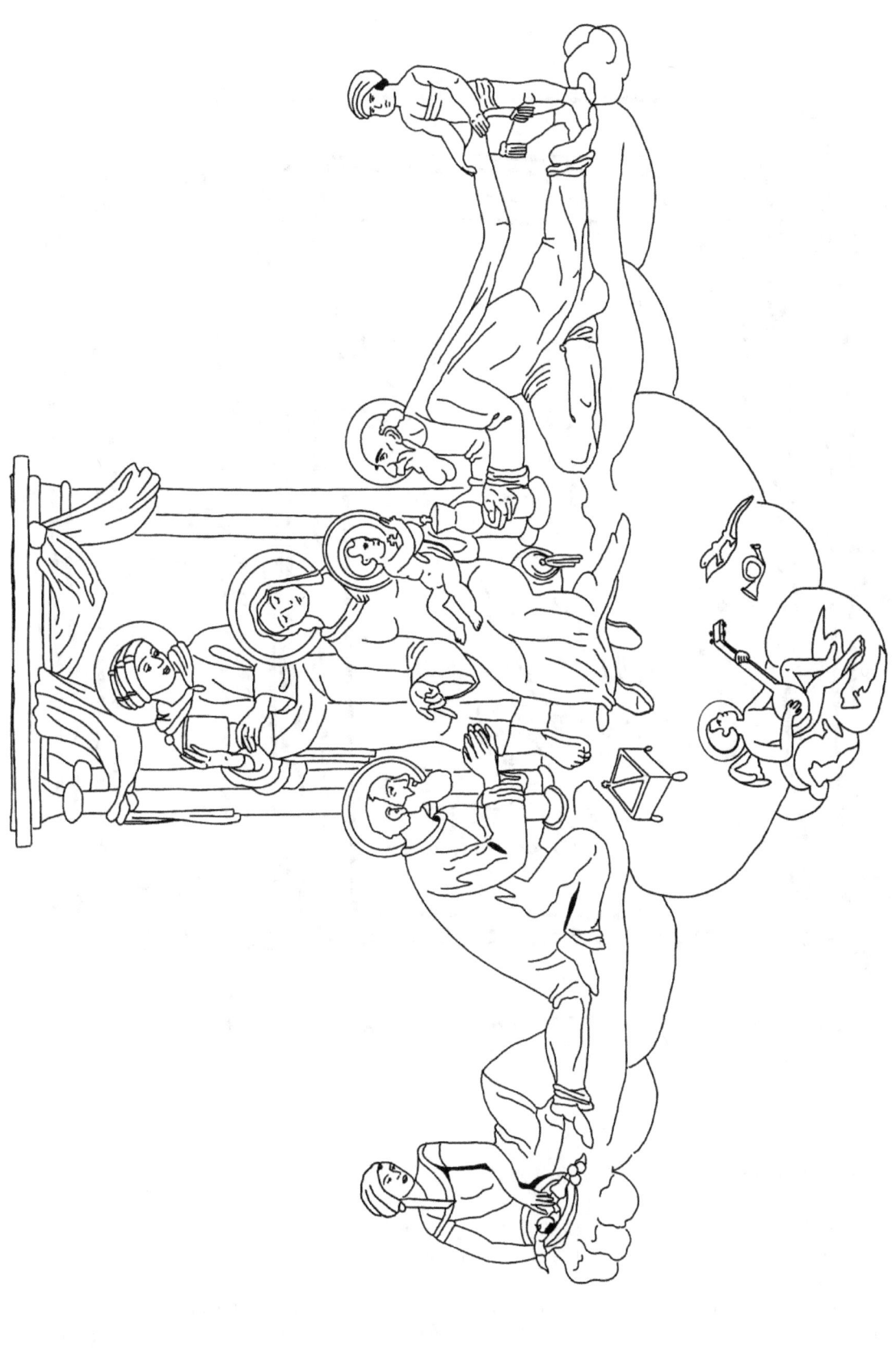

Am Kurpark 3, painted by Karl Gries around 1925

This large Lüftlmalerei depicts the Adoration of the Magi from the Gospel of Matthew. Although the Bible passage does not number or name the Magi, today we know them as Balthasar, Caspar, and Melchior. This trio of wise men are often depicted as kings, and, during the Renaissance, the youngest was frequently depicted as an African. Here, the artist painted the youngest, behind Mary and bearing a gift of myrrh, with definitively feminine features.

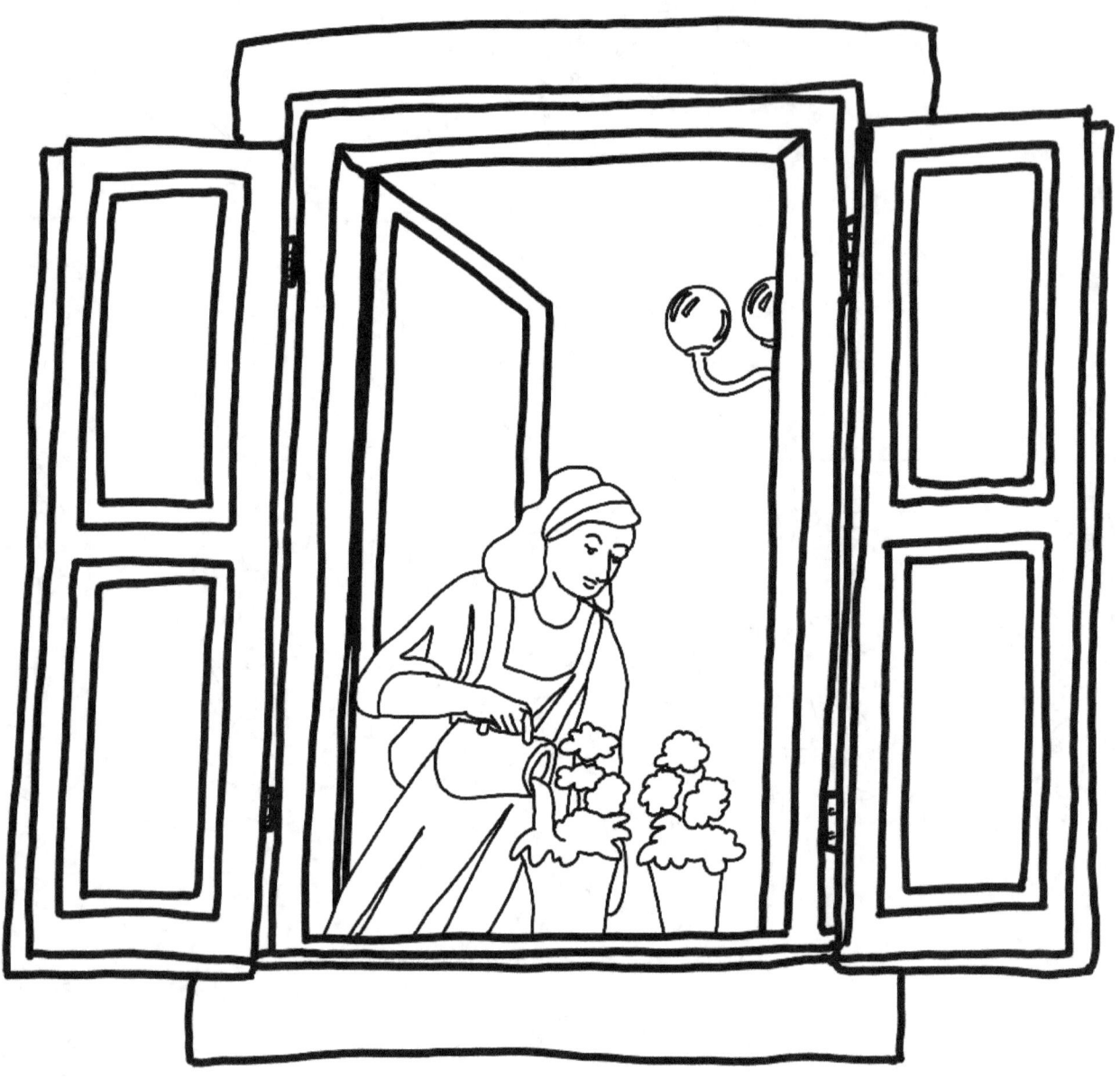

Am Kurpark 5, painted by an unknown artist in 1994

This Lüftlmalerei is a *Blind Window*, the term for when a blank wall is painted to look like a real window – even matching the size, shape, placement, shutters, and shadows of the actual windows on the building.

In Renaissance Italy, architects often incorporated Blind Windows in order to enrich or balance elaborate façades. This art of *fenestration*, or arranging windows for aesthetic purposes, sometimes took precedence over the practical purpose of actually providing air and light. (Not to be confused with *defenestration*, which means the act of throwing someone out of a window.)

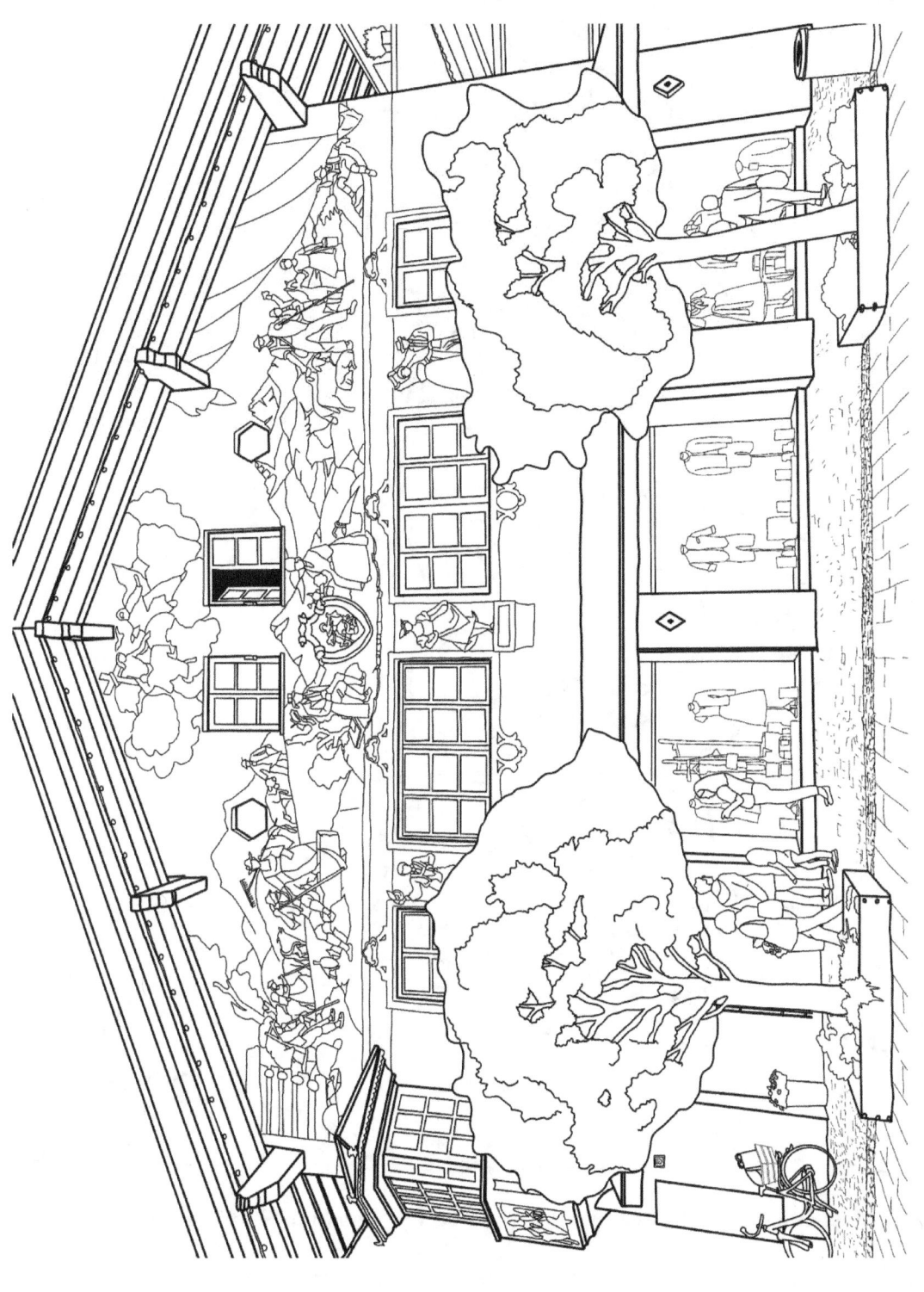

Trachten- und Modehaus Grasegger, Am Kurpark 8, painted by Sebastian Pfeffer in 1984

Trachten, from the German word *Tragen*, or "to wear," is the name for the traditional native dress in Bavaria. In 1883, when Josef Vogl (1848-1886) and five friends founded the first Association for the Preservation of Folk Costumes in Leitzachthal, there were no codified rules for traditional dress. Before that, "Trachten" were simply called "clothes." The first local Trachten preservation associations were formed in Partenkirchen in 1883, and in Garmisch in 1886. One hundred years later, Grasegger founded this clothing store, with the goal of selling stylish, contemporary clothes based on traditional Trachten. The building was covered in Lüftlmalerei of people wearing traditional costumes.

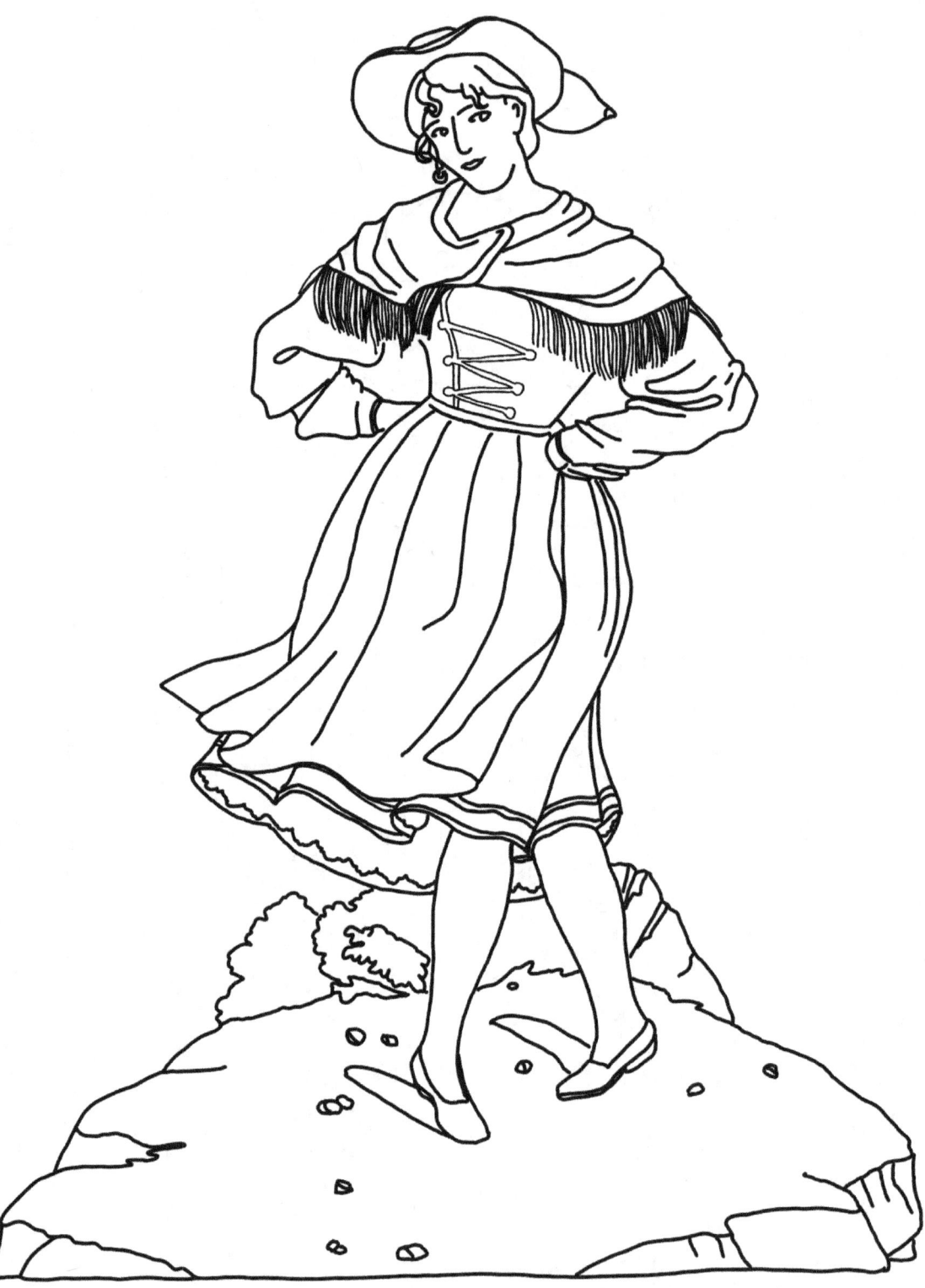

Trachten- und Modehaus Grasegger, Am Kurpark 8, painted by Sebastian Pfeffer in 1984

The word *Dirndl*, once an old Bavarian term for "little girl," has become the name for the traditional Bavarian women's costume. Originally the uniform for domestic servants in Bavaria in the 1800s called the *Dirndlgewand* (or, the "maid's dress"), traditional Dirndls consist of a bodice (*Mieder*), blouse (*Bluse*), a skirt (*Rock*), and an apron (*Schürze*). How the apron knot (the *Schleife*) is tied is said to reveal the wearer's availability. If the knot is on the left, she is single. If it's tied on the right, she's engaged or married. And if it's in the middle of her back, the wearer is either a widow – or a waitress.

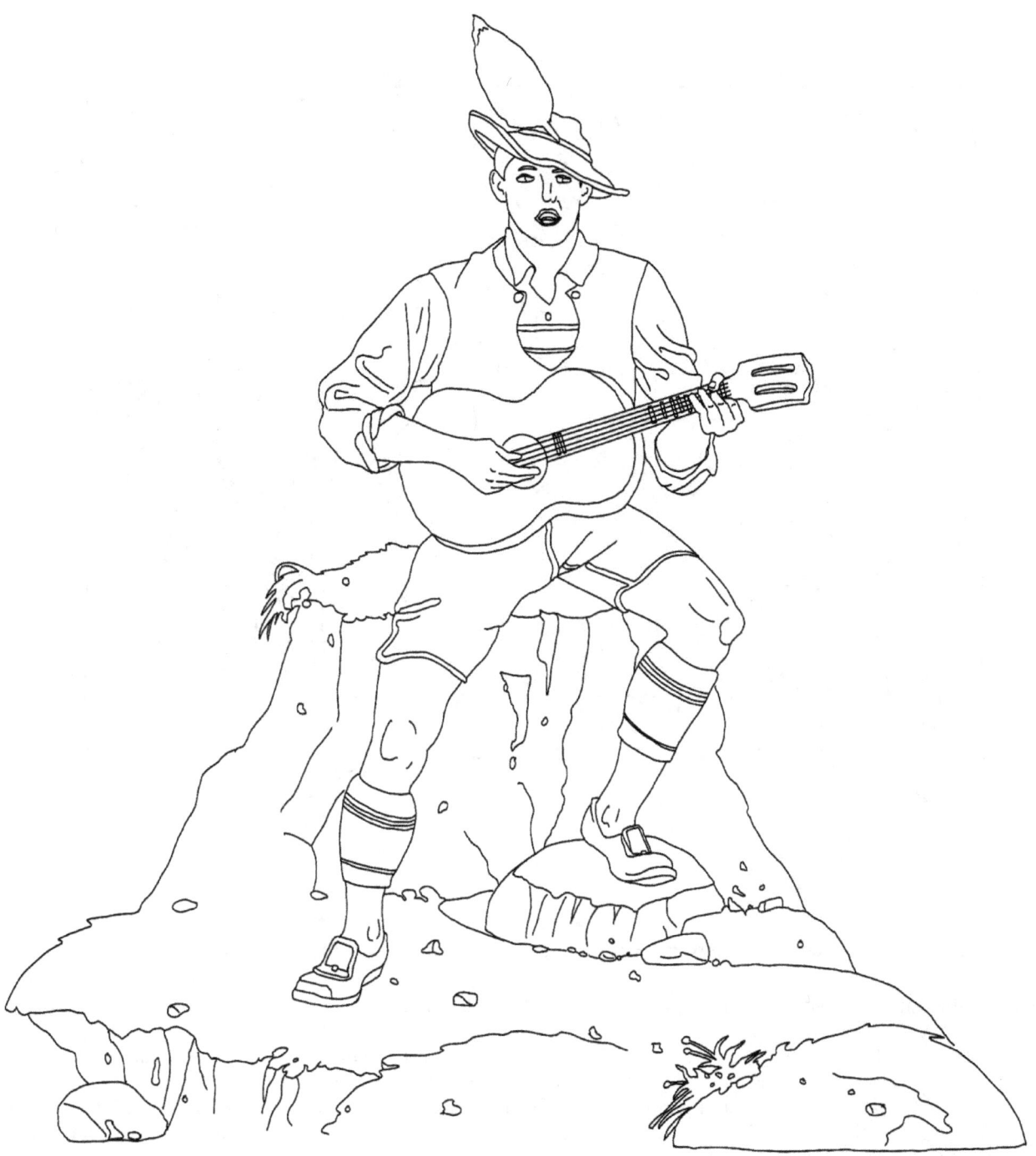

Trachten- und Modehaus Grasegger, Am Kurpark 8, painted by Sebastian Pfeffer in 1984

Lederhosen ("leather pants") are still traditionally worn by men in Bavaria on special occasions, such as weddings, or Oktoberfest. Lederhosen can be made of various types of leather, but buckskin, or deer hide, is the most popular. A complete Trachten outfit also includes the appropriate legwear – knitted calf-warmers known as *Loferl*, or *Pfousn* in Garmisch, or *Heaslan* in Partenkirchen.

Loferl – which may come from the German word *laufen*, which means "to walk" – are worn below the knee on the strongest part of the calf, leaving the ankle exposed.

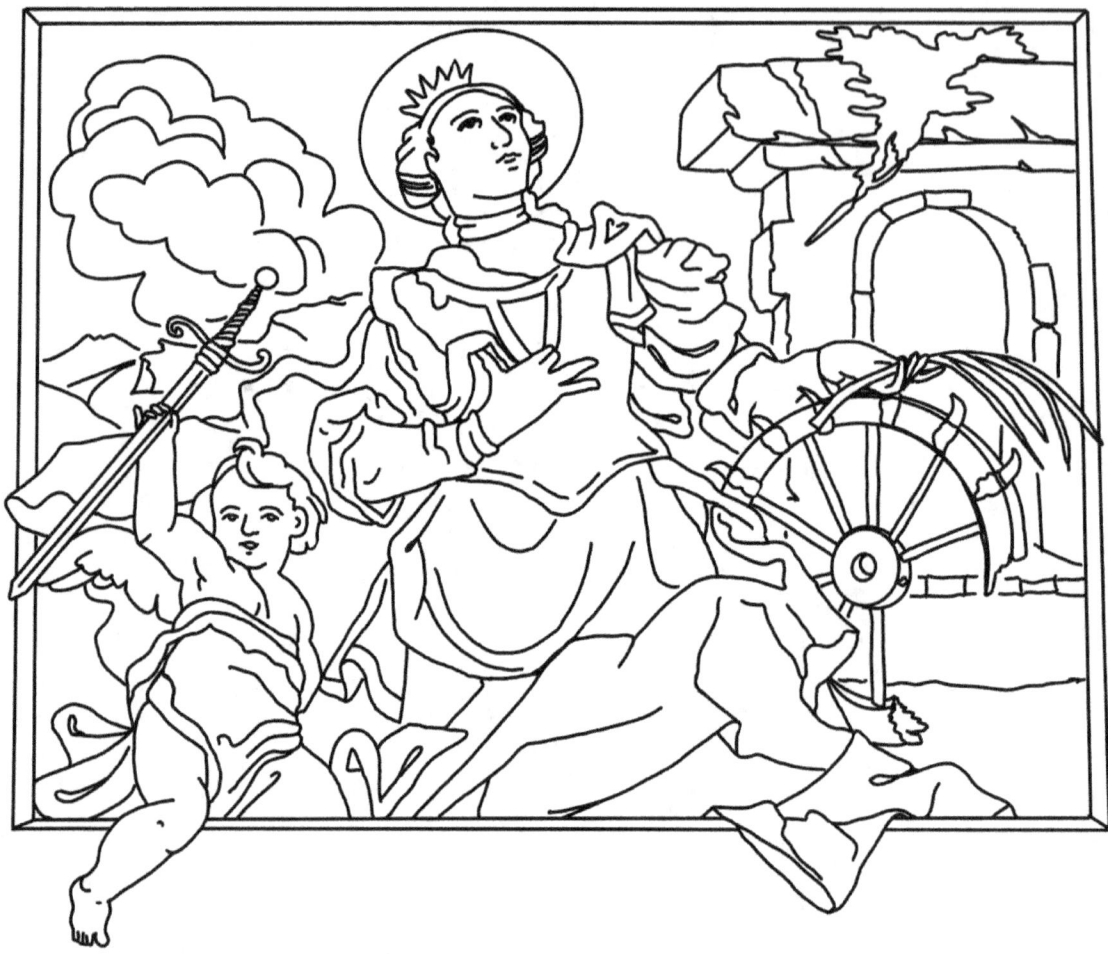

Trachten- und Modehaus Grasegger, Am Kurpark 8, painted by Sebastian Pfeffer in 1984

On the window on the corner of the building, a Lüftlmalerei of Saint Catherine.

Saint Catherine was the daughter of the governor of Alexandria during the reign of the Roman emperor Maximian (286–305). From a young age she devoted herself to study, and a vision of the Virgin Mary and infant Jesus is said to have persuaded her to become a Christian. When the Christian persecutions began under Maxentius, she was imprisoned and tortured. Catherine was condemned to death on a spiked breaking wheel, but, according to legend, at her touch, it was the wheel that miraculously shattered – not her.

In art, as here, Catherine is often depicted with a broken wheel. She also wears a crown, a symbol of her rank. In this image, Catherine is also holding a palm frond. During the time of the Romans, the palm frond was a symbol of victory. That carried over into Christian symbolism, where palm fronds came to denote a martyr's victory over death.

A sword often denotes that the saint suffered martyrdom at the edge of a blade. Here, an angel is holding a sword aloft beside the saint in the Lüftlmalerei, and, as the story of Saint Catherine goes, when the wheel failed to break her, Maxentius then ordered her beheaded.

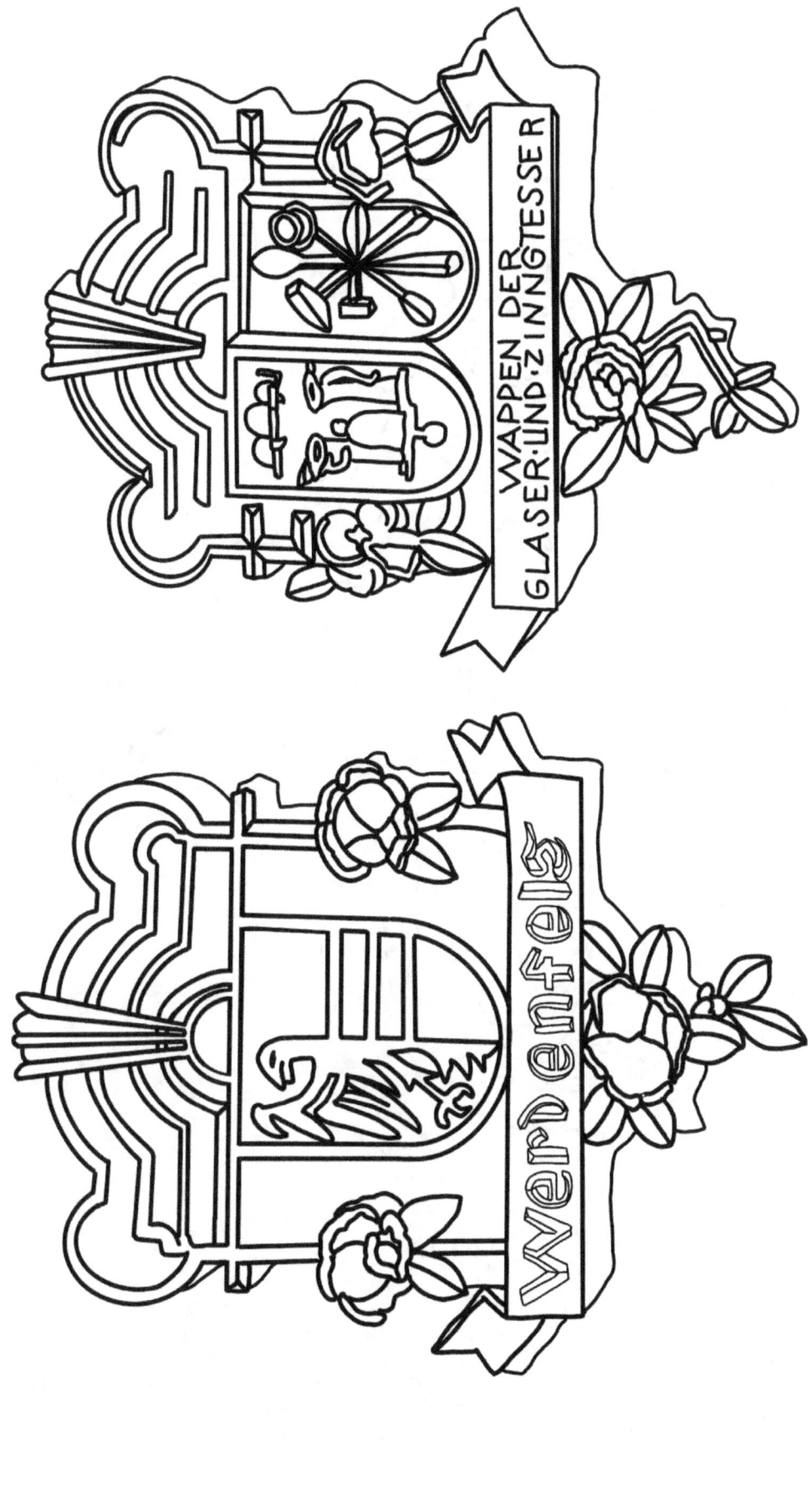

Original site of the Dersch family Glaserei, Am Kurpark 11, painted by Heinrich Bickel around 1928

The Lüftlmalerei here are pictures of coats of arms designating this building's history as the original site of the Dersch family glazier, or glass craft shop.

One, the coat of arms of Werdenfels County. At its center, the coat of arms of the Counts of Eschenlohe, who had once been the lords of the County of Werdenfels, which had its seat at the Werdenfels Castle on a hill overlooking Garmisch-Partenkirchen. This symbol was adopted by the newly combined town of Garmisch-Partenkirchen when they were merged together in 1935.

The other, a combination of coats of arms. On the left, the symbol for a pewter smith with a forged bell in the center and silver mugs at the sides. On the right, the symbol for the glass glazier's trade with its ancient tools, a glass cutter, glazier's hammer, and soldering iron.

9

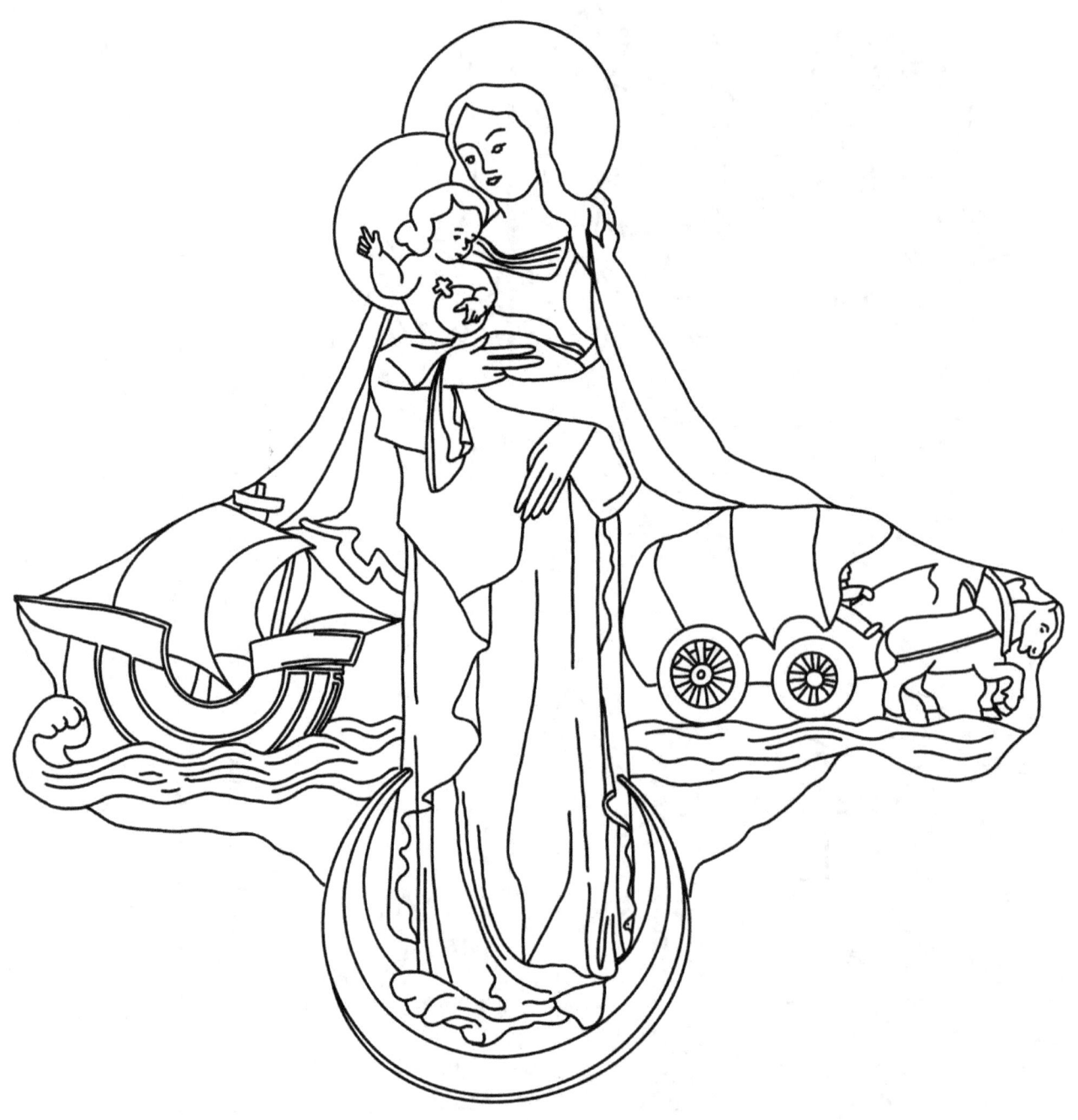

Am Kurpark 13, originally painted by Karl Gries around 1925

An image of the Patrona Bavaria as patron of trade and porters. Mary as the patron saint of Bavaria (*Patrona Bavariae* in Latin) was first established by Maximilian I (1573-1651) while Duke of Bavaria. In 1616, he had a bronze statue made labeled the "Patrona Boiariae." In the statue, Mary stands with her foot on the crescent moon, with a scepter in her one hand and holding Christ in the other, who, himself holds a globus cruciger (or a cross-topped orb) as a sign of his sovereignty over everything. The statue was fashioned after the vision in the Revelation of John of "a woman clothed with the sun, with the moon under her feet and a crown of twelve stars on her head." (Rev 12:1). However, there are no stars in the Lüftlmalerei here.

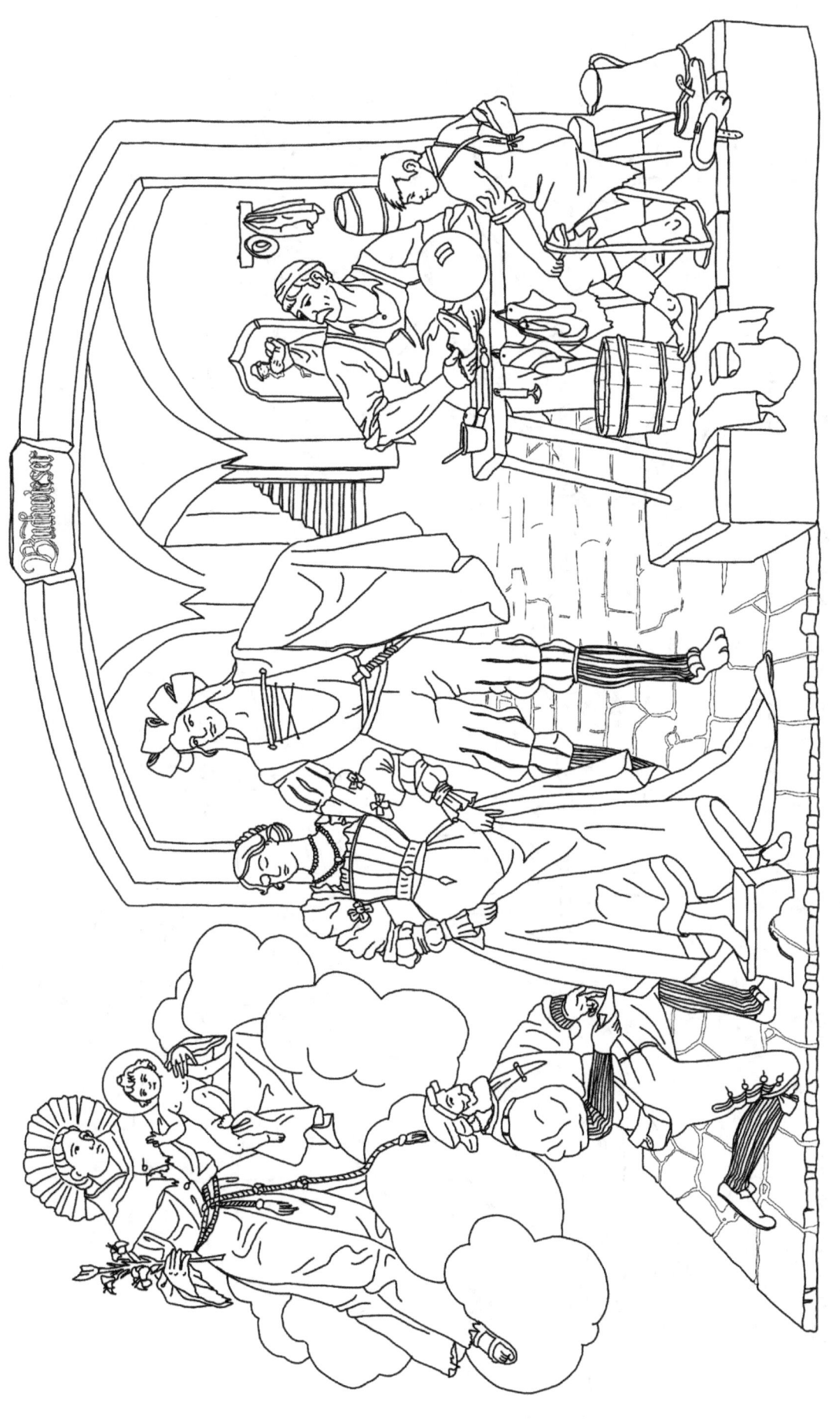

Anton Buchwieser's Shoe Store, Am Kurpark 14, painted by Sebastian Pfeffer in 1984

On the wall outside Anton Buchwieser's shoe store, a large narrative Lüftlmalerei depicting the owner's name saint, Saint Anthony (Anton in German), and a scene from Richard Wagner's opera Die Meistersinger von Nürnberg ("The Master Singer from Nuremberg"). The opera features Hans Sachs (1494–1576), perhaps the most famous cobblers in all of German history, depicted here kneeling below Saint Anthony. Sachs, who was a shoemaker by profession, was also a *Meistersinger* ("Master Singer"), and prolific poet and playwright – having written some 6,000 unique works during his lifetime.

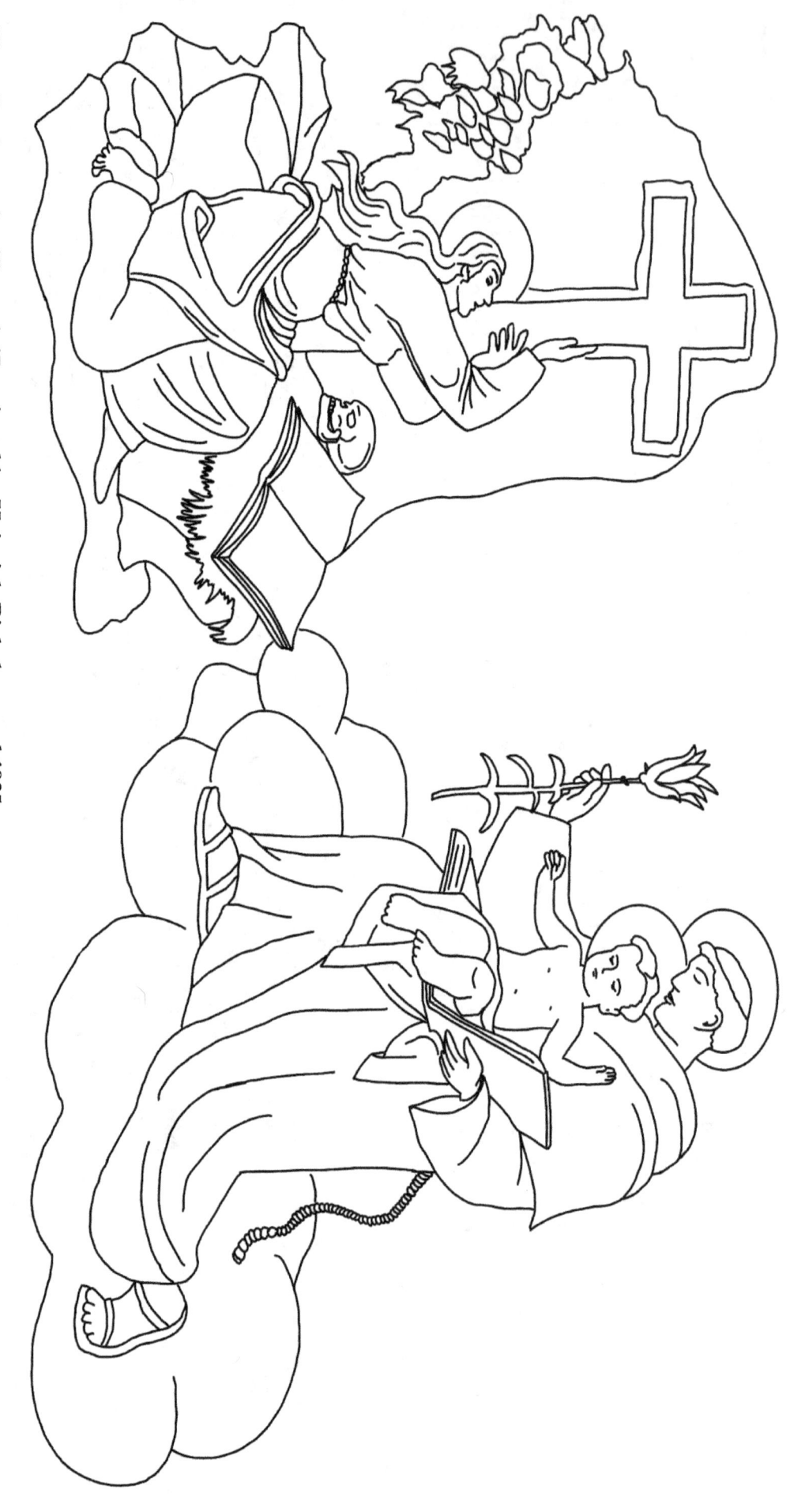

Haus Gattinger, Am Kurpark 17, painted by Heinrich Bickel around 1935

On the left, an image of Mary Magdalene, a woman who, according to the gospels, traveled with Jesus as one of his followers and was a witness to his crucifixion and its aftermath. In "The Penitent Magdalene," a 1565 painting by Titian, the artist first introduced an open book and a skull as a *memento mori*, or an object depicting the inevitability of death, in images of the saint.

On the right, an image of Saint Anthony, patron saint of lost things and the patron saint of the nearby pilgrimage church in Partenkirchen. Saint Anthony is often portrayed, as here, with a lily, a book, and, especially after the Renaissance, he came to be represented as carrying the Christ Child.

The two saints commemorate the former owners, Anton Gattinger, and his wife, Magdelena.

12

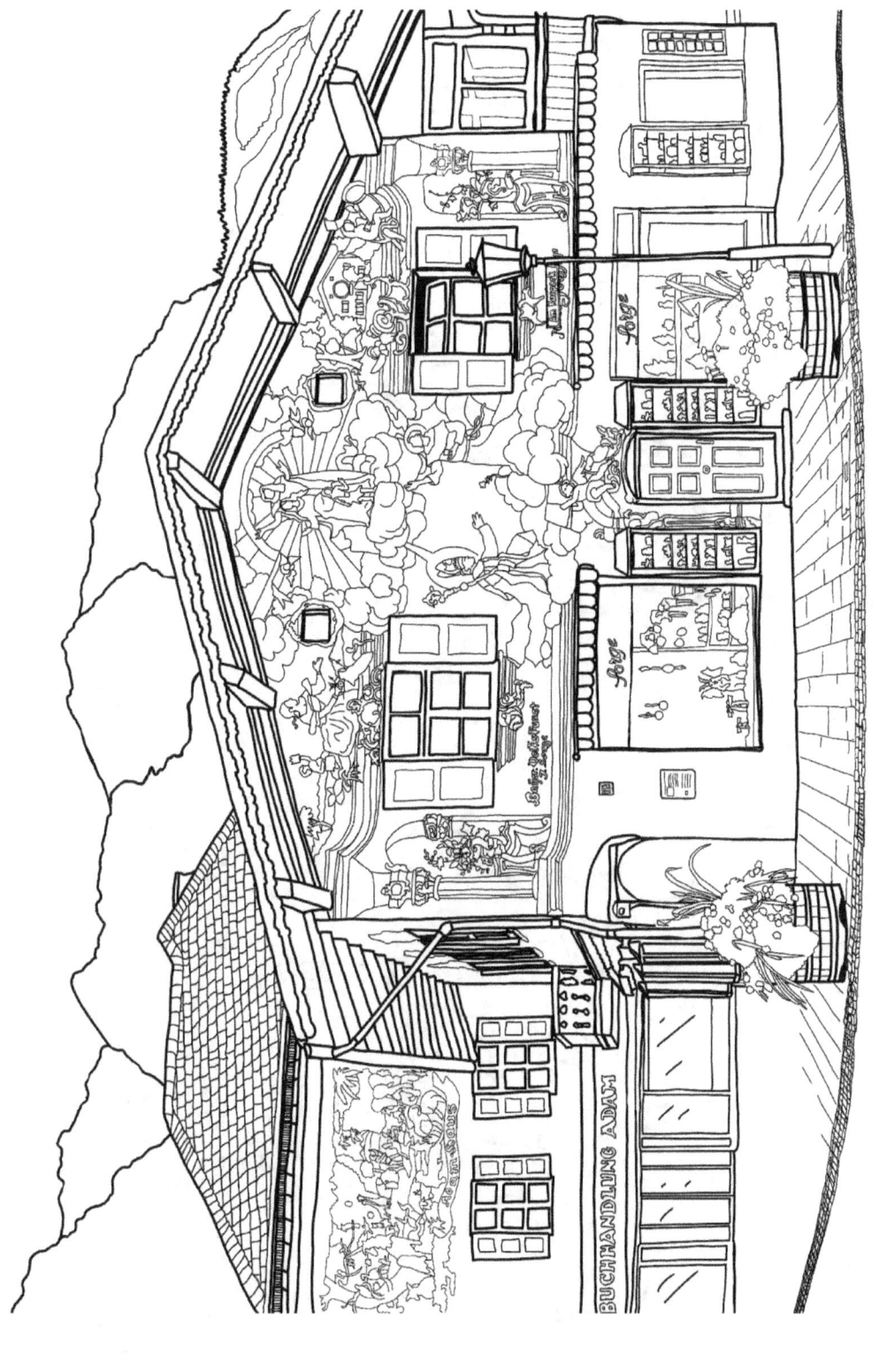

Sorge & Geschwister's souvenir shop, Am Kurpark 18, painted by Heinrich Bickel in 1926

In 1760, this one-time Garmisch town hall, with a requisite dance hall on the second floor, was sold to Stephan Jocher — hence the "Haus Jocher" painted beneath the window on the right. His grandson, Johann Georg, who went by the name "Schloapferer," gave the building its current title, the "zum Schloapferer" House, noted on a scroll behind the *putto* at the bottom. For the last three generations, the Sorge family has run the store here selling "Bayer Volkskunst" (or the "Bavarian Folk Art") that you see today. Joseph "Max" Jocher commissioned the local artist Heinrich Bickel to incorporate the building's history into his mural on the front, including an image of Saint Elisabeth in the top left corner of the gable, and in the top right corner, a reference to this building when it was still a dance hall, with a *putto* and musical instruments beside an image of the building and its original Lüftlmalerei.

13

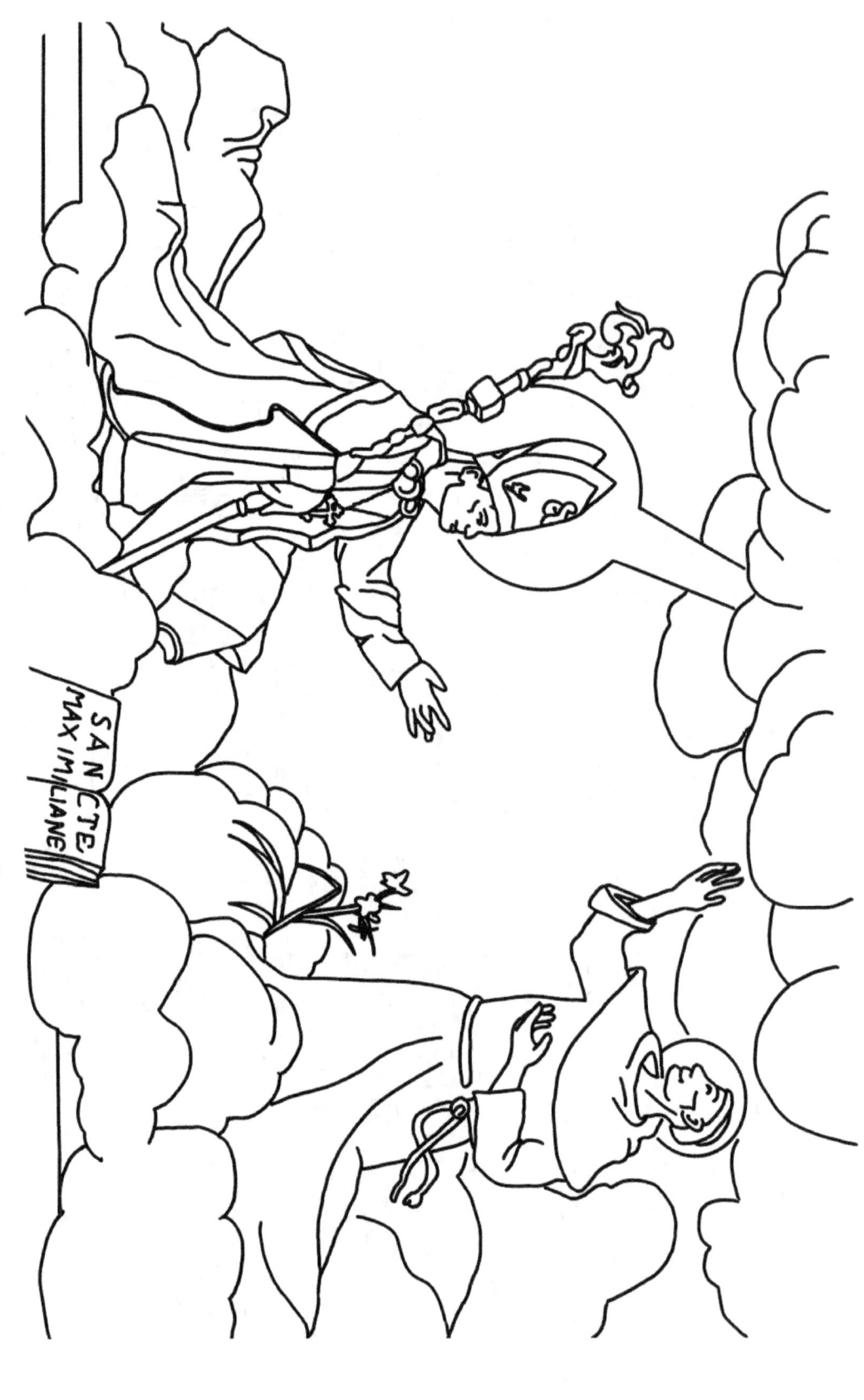

Sorge & Geschwister's souvenir shop, Am Kurpark 18, painted by Heinrich Bickel in 1926

The owner at the time the Lüftlmalerei was painted, Joseph "Max" Jocher's name saint, Saint Maximilian, Bishop of Lorch, is prominently situated in the center of the mural. *Maximilians* (meaning "The Greatest" in Latin) was an apostle to what is now Austria and Slovenia in the 3rd century. According to local legend, he is apocryphally credited with establishing the first Christian church in Freising near what is now the city of Munich, converting an old pagan temple into a church dedicated to the Virgin Mary.

At the right, an image of Saint Anthony of Padua, the patron saint of lost things and of the nearby Saint Anthony pilgrimage church.

14

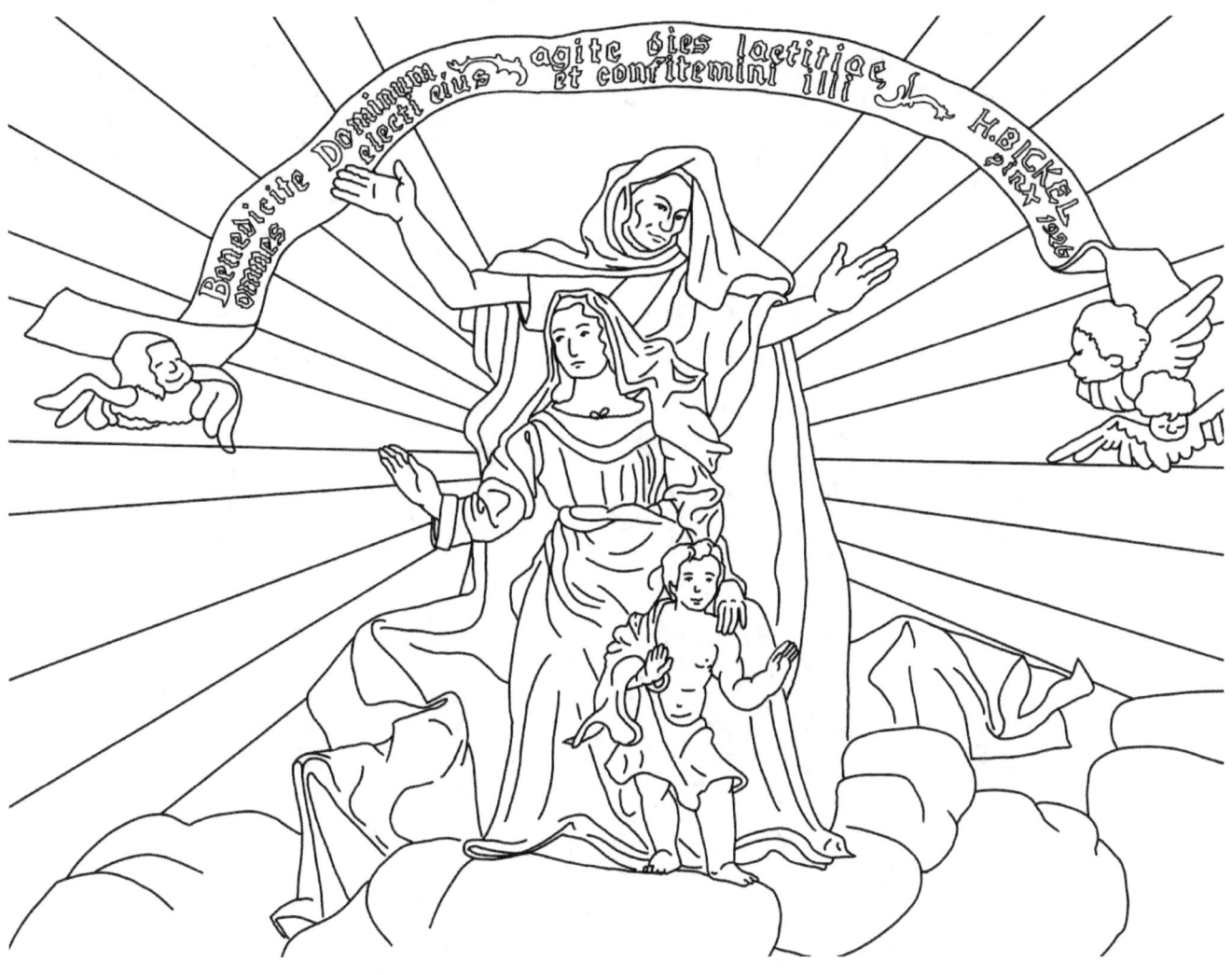

Sorge & Geschwister's souvenir shop, Am Kurpark 18, painted by Heinrich Bickel in 1926

In the center, an image of Saint Anne, Mary's mother, with Mary and Jesus. Named an *Anna Selbdritt*, this sort of depiction of Jesus's female family forming a feminine trinity has been popular in Germany since the 14th century. The banner above is a line from the Book of Tobit 13:10 in Latin: "Benedicite Dominum omnes electi eius agite dies laetitiae et confitemini illi" ("Give praise to the Lord, for he is good"), as well as the word *Pinx*, a Latin abbreviation for "painted by," "Bickel," and the date.

Around them float body-less cherubim. In Baroque art, a cherub was often represented as only the head of an infant between a pair of wings – a figure termed a *Cherub's Head*. Artists meant them to be emblematic of a pure spirit, the head representing the soul, love, and intelligence.

Adam Bookstore, Am Kurpark 20, painted by Heinrich Bickel in 1930

For almost 100 years, the Adam Printing Press published tourist guides and books focused on tourism to the Garmisch-Pattenkirchen region. Today, while the publisher has since closed, the Adam Bookstore remains.

Above the front door, in a nod to the name of the printer, "Adam," a large Lüftlmalerei inspired by the works of Jan Brueghel the Elder of Adam and Eve in the Garden of Eden titled "Paradise."

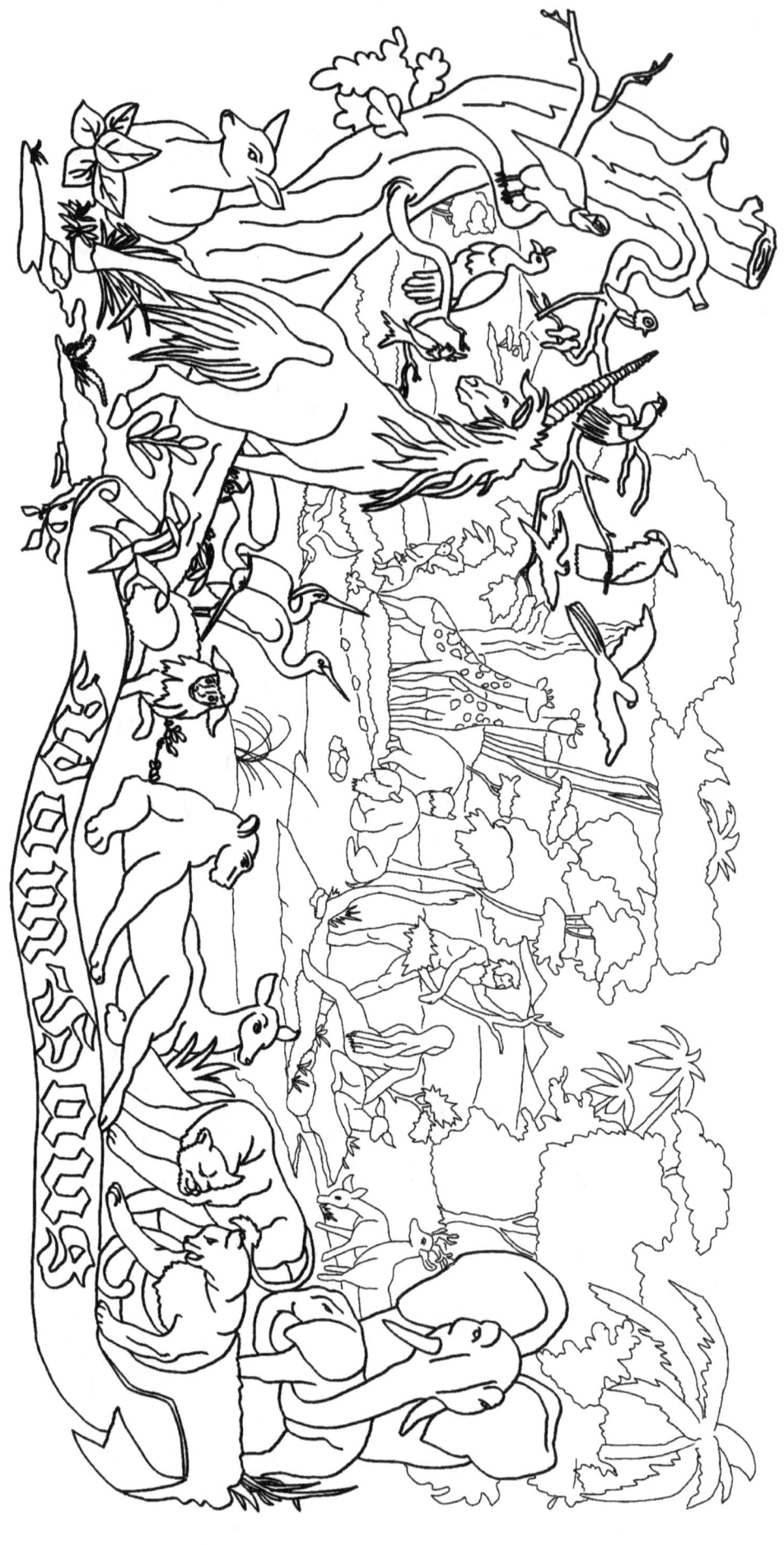

16

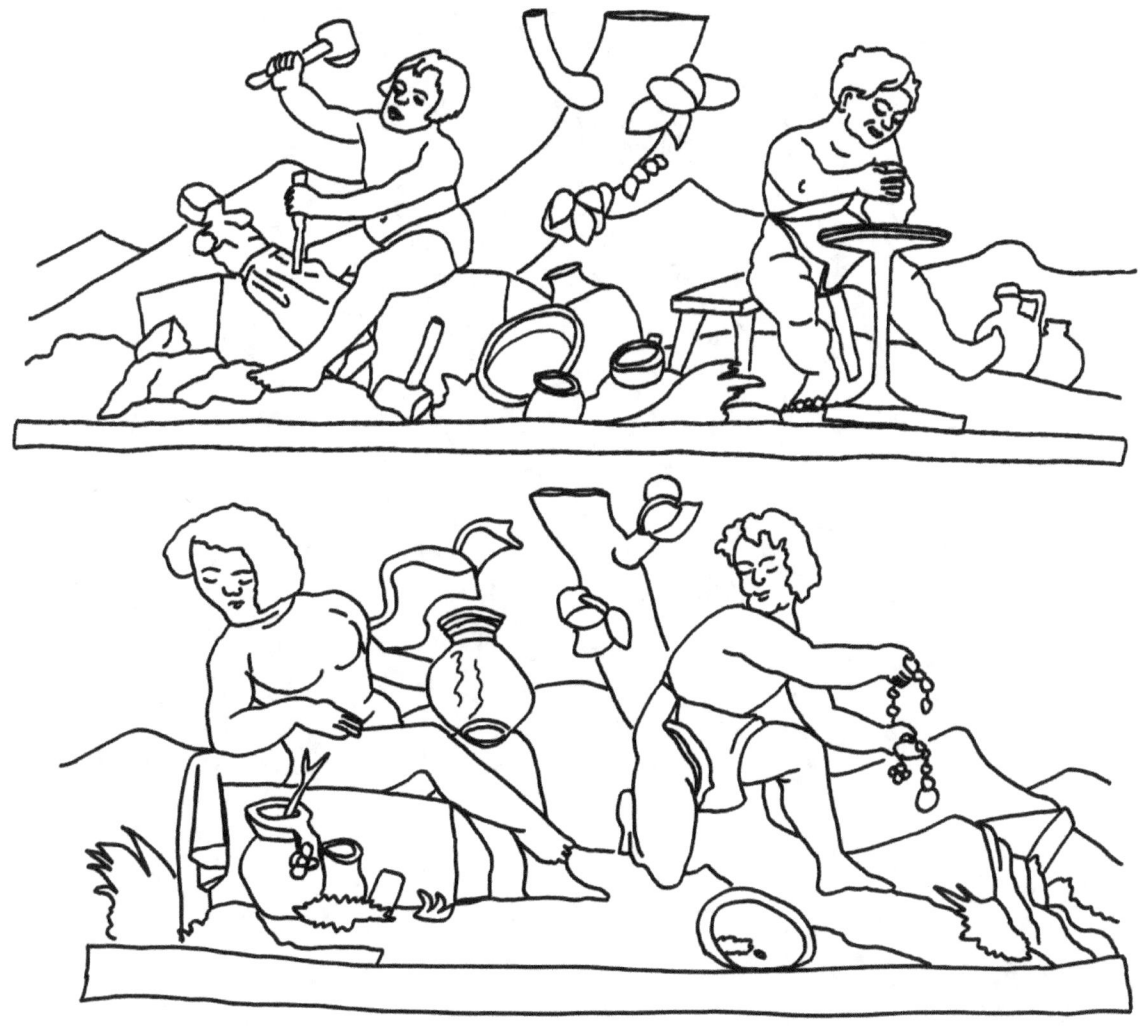

Former Sorge family residence, Am Kurpark 25, painted by Heinrich Bickel in 1931

A *putto* is the name for the chubby child figure, often depicted with wings, frequently appearing in both mythological and religious art from the Renaissance – like Cupid, for example.

The wingless and rather muscular putti here work in all the positions of medieval craftsmen: a sculptor, a potter with his wheel, a glazer painting pots, and a jeweler making a necklace – fitting symbols on the wall of this former handcrafted souvenir selling family's home.

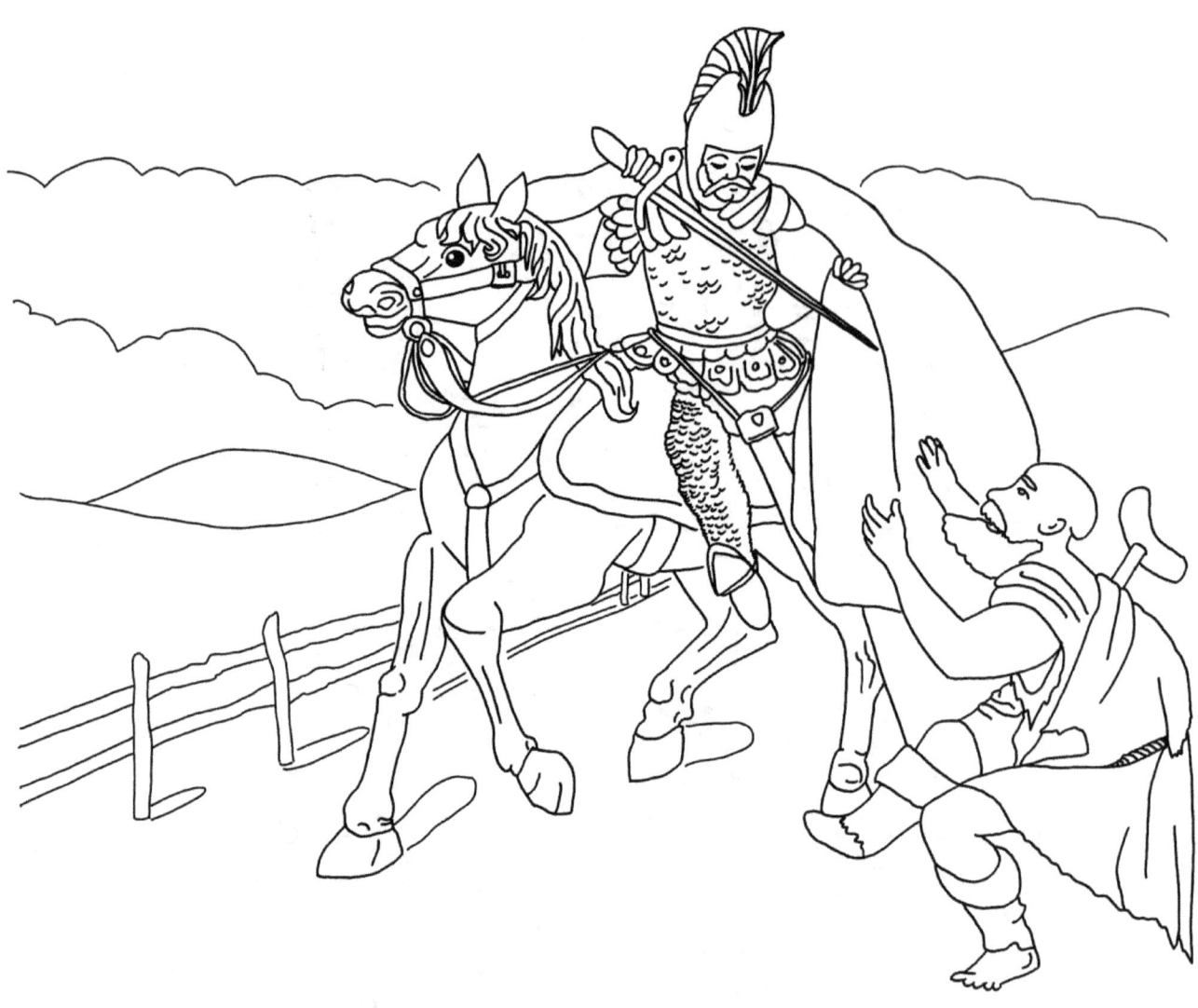

Am Kurpark 25, painted by Gerhard Ester around 1990

Saint Martin is the patron saint and symbol of Garmisch. Born in 336 AD, legend has it that Martin, a Roman cavalry soldier stationed in Gaul (now Amiens, France), used his sword to cut his own cloak to give half to a beggar. That night, the beggar revealed himself to Martin in a dream to have been Jesus Christ, and Martin awoke to find his cloak made whole again.

The supposed relic of Saint Martin's miraculous cloak was kept in an Abbey near Tours, France. The priest who cared for the cloak in its reliquary was called a *cappellanu* in Latin, and ultimately all priests who served in the military were called *cappellani*. The French translation is *chapelains*, from which the English word "chaplain" is derived.

A similar linguistic development took place for the term for the small church built for the relic. Once known as a *capella*, or "a little cloak," eventually, small churches lost their association with the actual cloak and with the original Latin, and all small Christian churches began to be referred to as "chapels" – which is how they're known today.

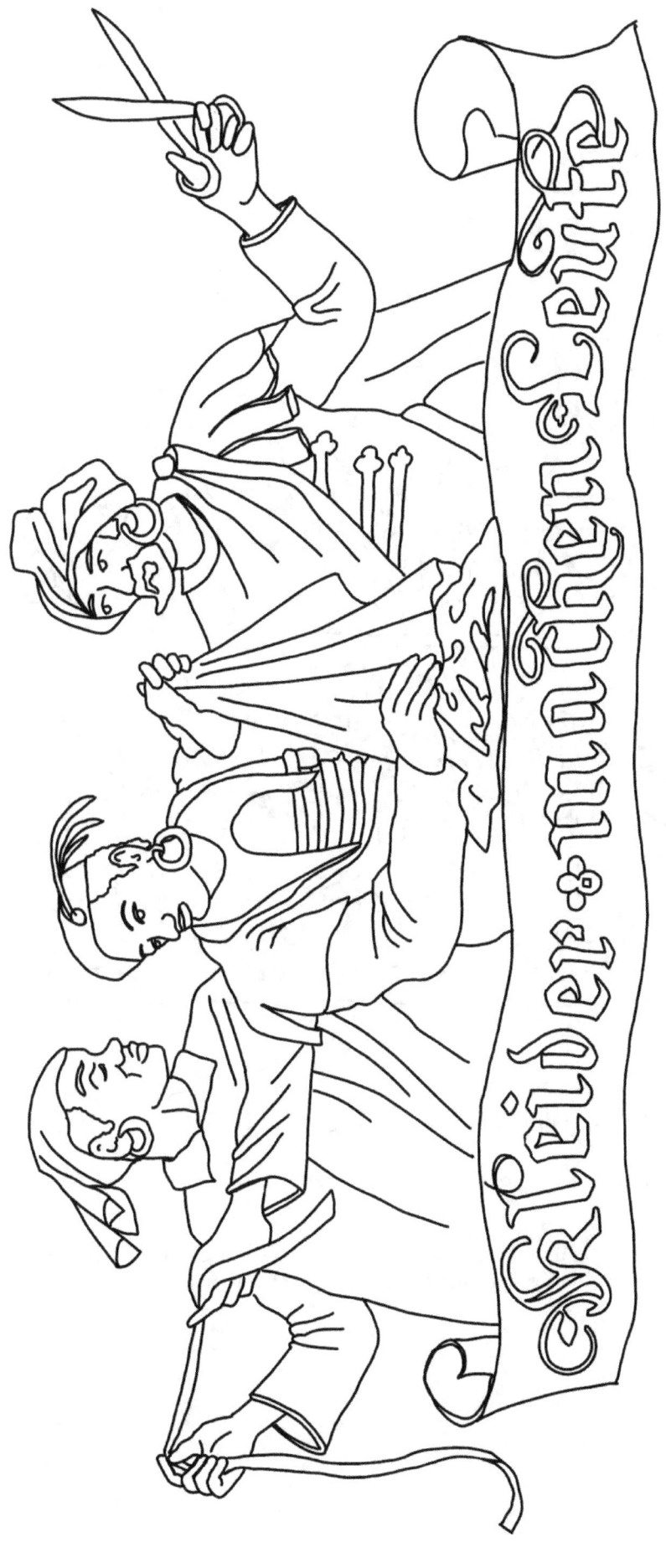

Mohrenplatz 7, painted by Franz Winterholler in 1984

Mohrenplatz, or "Moors' Square," was named in 1927 for the Hotel Drei Mohren ("Three Moors") which, for nearly 100 years, stood at what is now Mohrenplatz 7.

In the 1880s, Joseph Reiser managed the Hotel Gasthaus zu den drei Mohren on Ludwigstraße in what was then the nearby and separate town of Partenkirchen. In 1890, he expanded and established the Hotel Drei Mohren here in Garmisch. However, the hotel closed in 1978.

Today, as a remnant of that once eponymous hotel, there is still a Lüftlmalerei of three Moors holding tailor's tools, and the banner beneath them says: "Kleider machen Leute," or "Clothes maketh the Man" – advertising, while at the same time harkening back, to a clothing store that took the place of the Hotel.

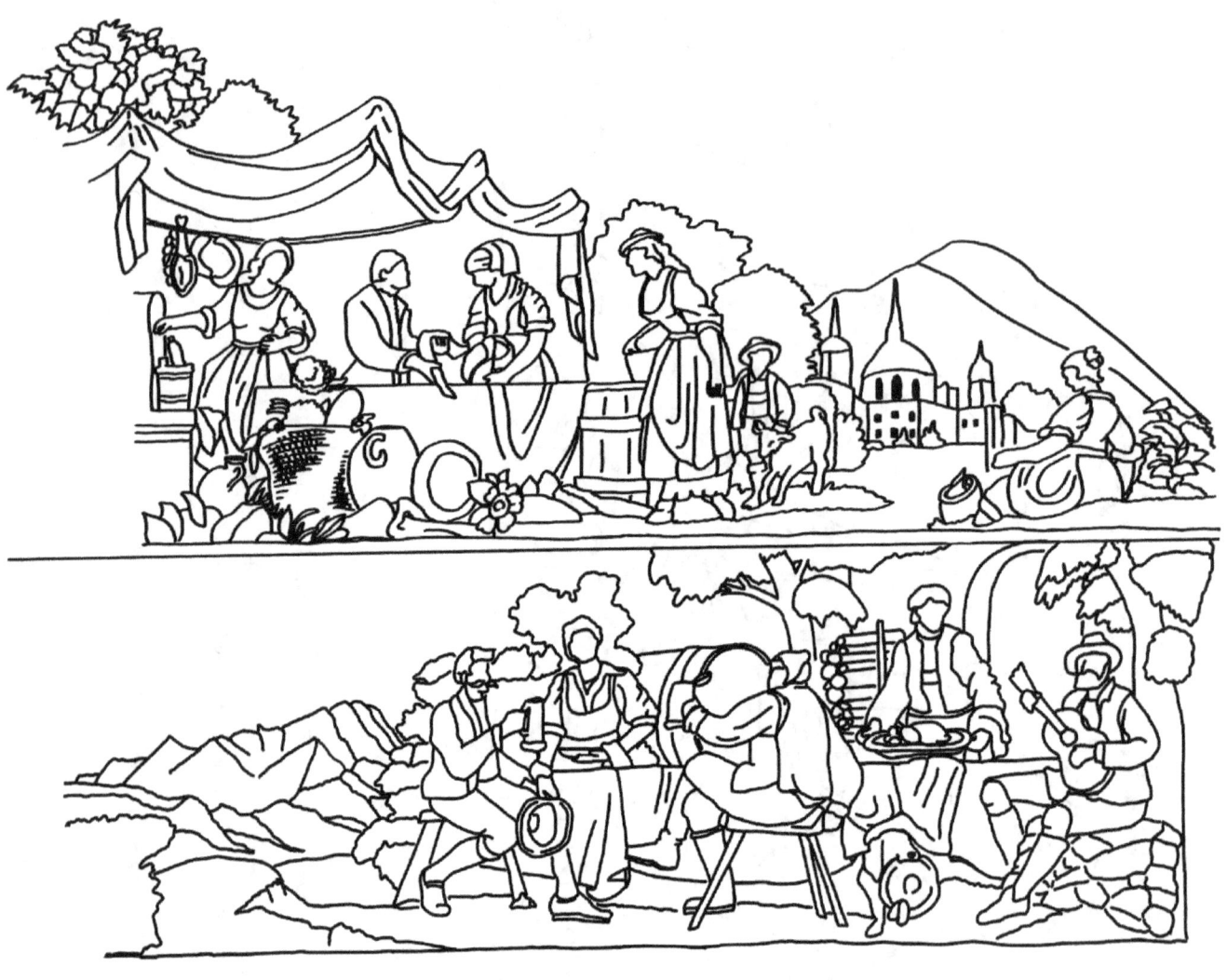

Fischer's Mohrenplatz Inn, Mohrenplatz 4, painted by Rainer Wagner in 2008

The Lüftlmalerei in the gable of Fischer's Mohrenplatz Inn depicts the owner, Andreas Fischer's family history and his restaurant's place in Garmisch-Partenkirchen.

On one side, a medieval market scene with the Abbey in the nearby village of Ettal near Oberammergau in the background. The fish seller in the market stall is the owner, Andreas Fischer, himself, whose family has roots in Ettal.

On the opposite side, a Bavarian tavern with the Wetterstein Mountains in the background, representing Fischer's restaurant here in Garmisch, which sells fresh, regional food.

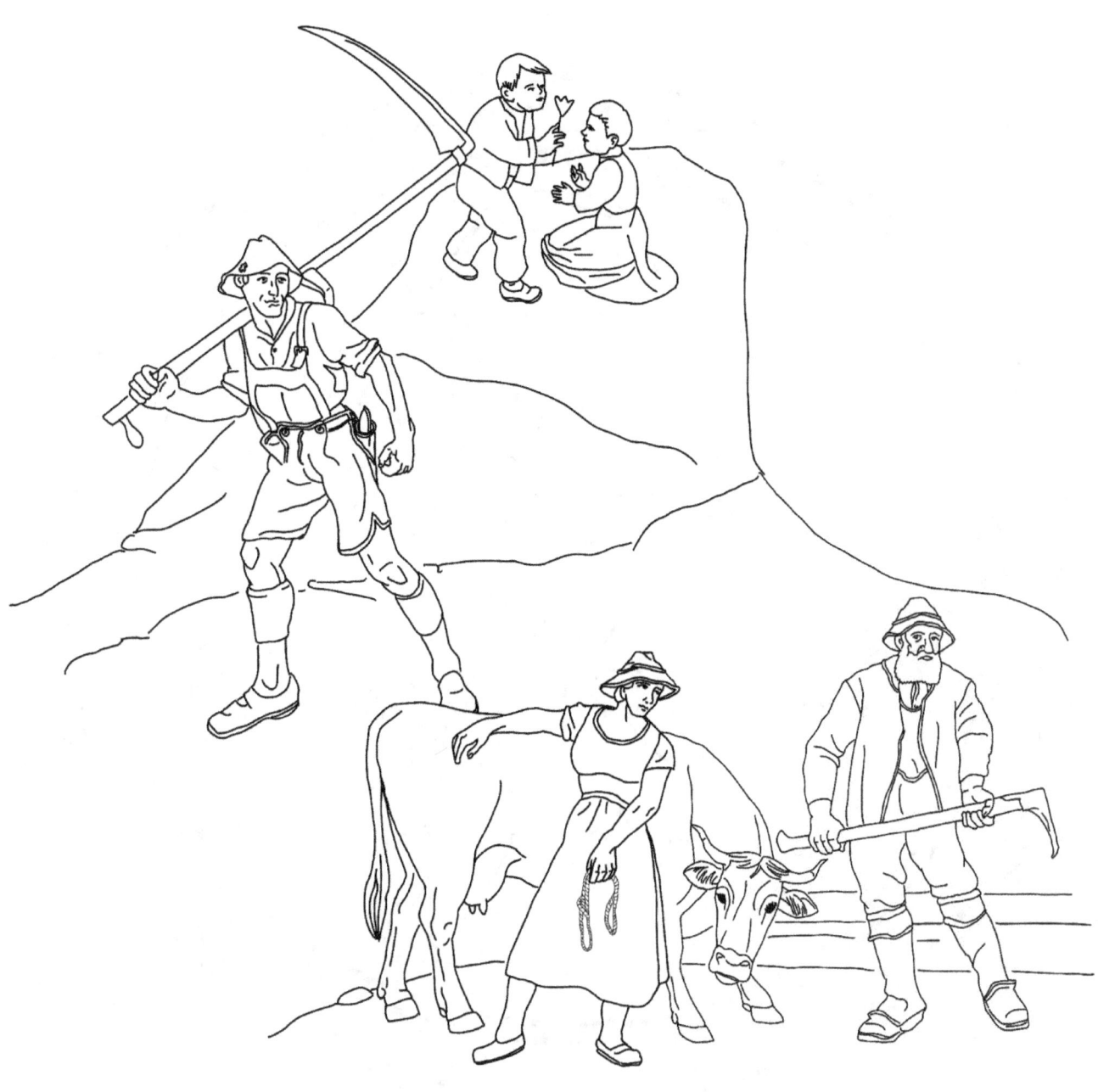

Mohrenplatz 1, first painted by Heinrich Bickel in 1935, restored by Sebastian Pfeffer in 1997

In this mural, titled an "Allegory of Ages," the artist depicts the stages of a local farmer's life: first as a child picking flowers, then as a young man working in the fields, and, finally, as an old man still hard at work.

The style of this restored Lüftlmalerei is an amalgam of the two most prolific fresco painters in Garmisch-Partenkirchen, a blend of the Baroque romanticism of the original local artist Heinrich Bickel, whose work promoted the virtue of the working man and peasant farmer, and the colorful attention to detail and contemporary style of Sebastian Pfeffer from nearby Mittenwald.

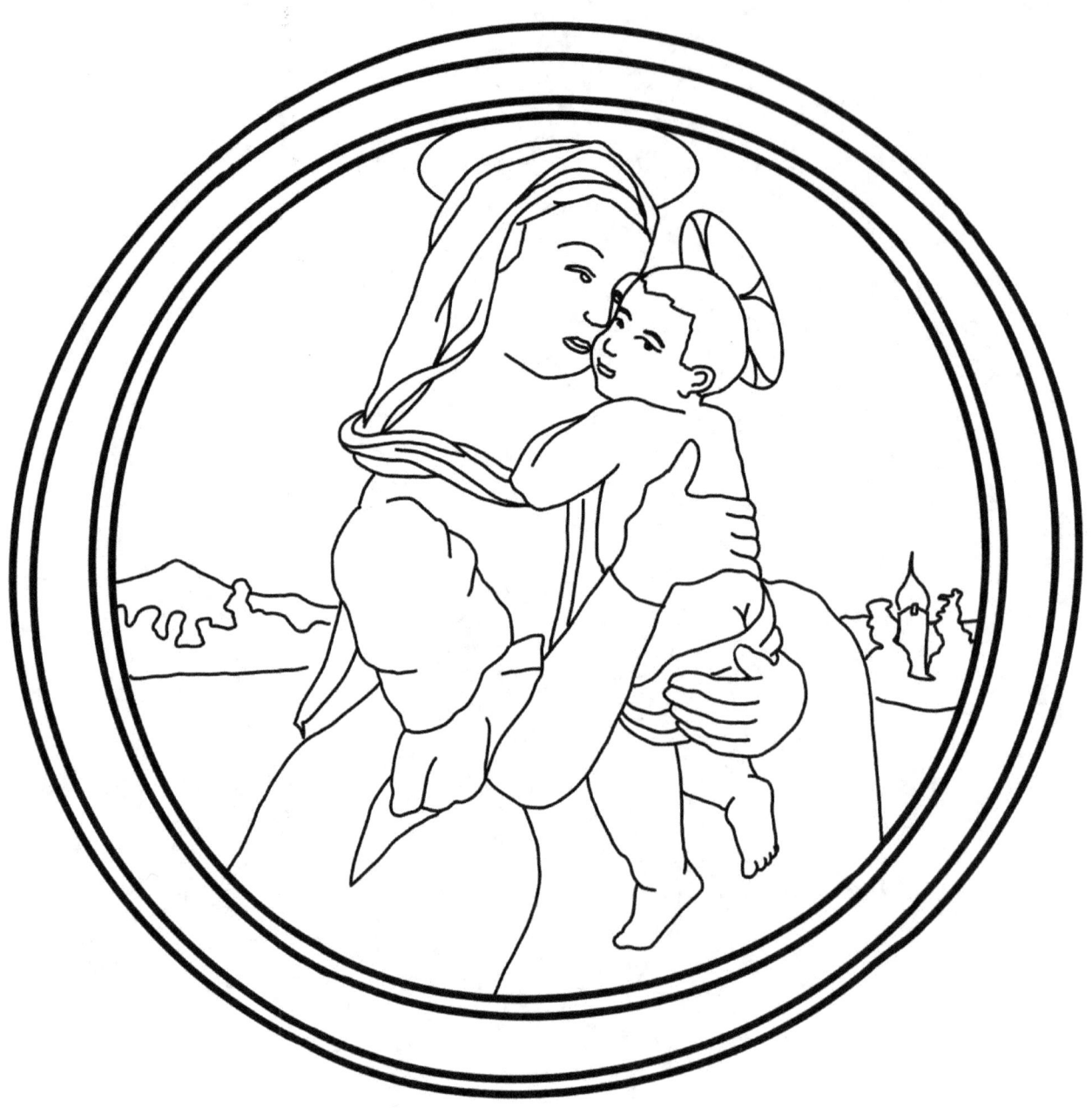

Marienplatz 2a, painted by Heinrich Bickel in 1932

The Garmisch market square was renamed *Marienplatz* ("Mary's Square") for the war memorial built here in 1922, a statue of the Patrona Bavaria.

No image is more prevalent in Christendom (aside from the image of Jesus on the cross) than that of the Virgin Mary with an infant Christ. Mary is frequently portrayed, as here, the merciful mother, as the very personification of grace, gathering together all humanity in her maternal embrace. This picture is often called the *Mater Amabilis*, Latin for the "Mother Worthy of Love."

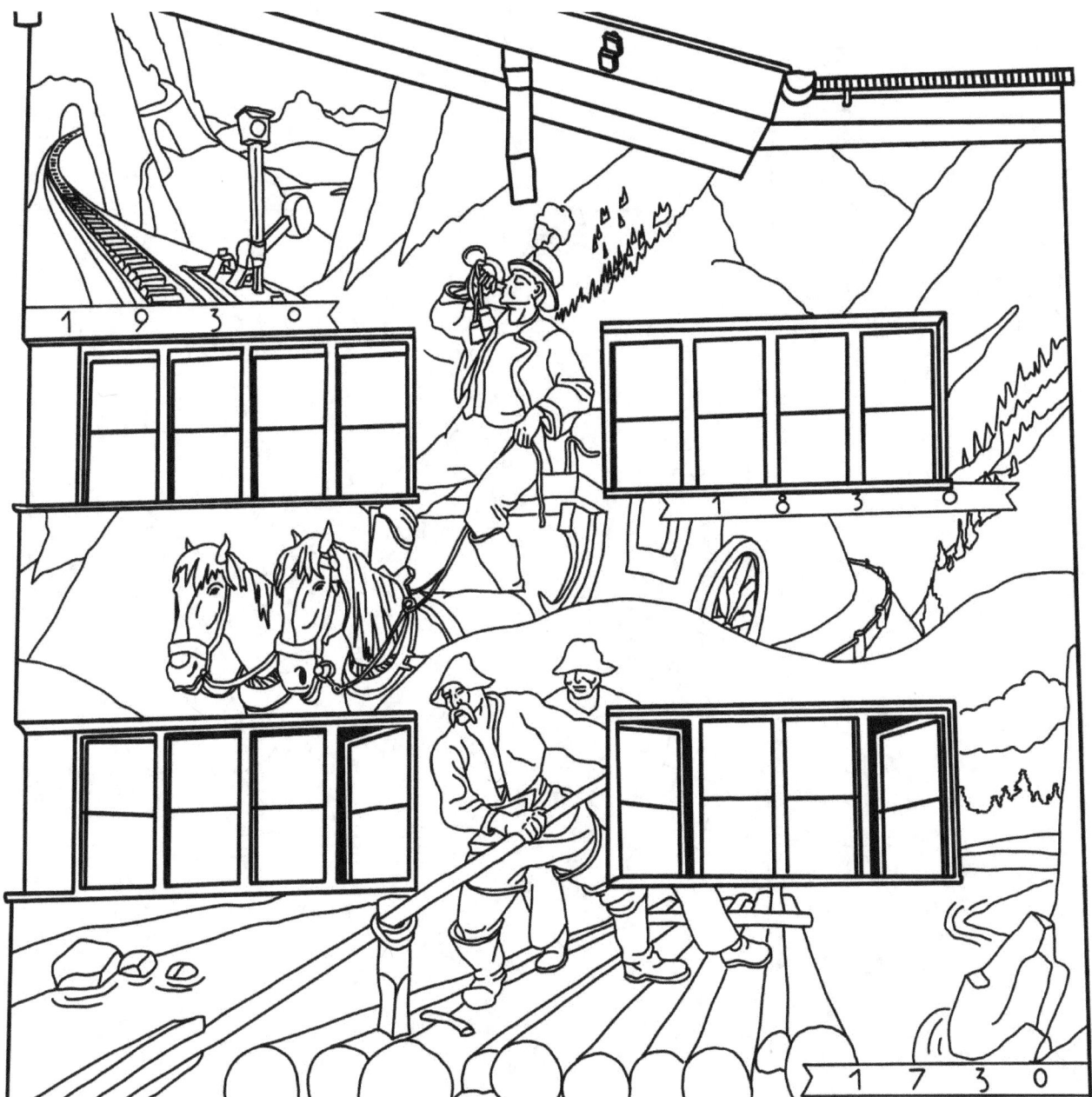

Former Zugspitzbahn ticket office, Marienplatz 5, painted by Heinrich Bickel in 1933

On the front of the building, a large Lüftlmalerei shows the advancement of travel through Garmisch-Partenkirchen over the last three centuries.

Starting at the bottom, in "1730," Bickel painted men traveling down the Loisach river on a raft made of roughhewn logs. In the 1700s, lumber from the nearby mountains was floated down the river by brave raftsmen. Adopting the idyllic style of Albin Egger-Lienz's "Two Mountain Mowers" (1913), Bickel depicts these men as primevally powerful mountain men.

Next, in the center, in "1830," a *Postillion*, a postman, travels down the road on a horse drawn carriage while blowing a horn. Postillions wore uniformed clothing and carried a post trumpet – now the symbol for the German postal system. The horn made it clear that the Postillion had priority when using traffic routes, ferries, and bridges. In the 1800s, Postillions were "posted" to and paid by Post Hotels.

Finally, at the top, "1930," the Zugspitzbahn railway, which first went into operation on February 19, 1929. The line, still in operation today, runs from the center of Garmisch-Partenkirchen to the Zugspitzplatt on the Zugspitze mountain, 2.6 kilometers above sea level, making it the highest railway in Germany and the third highest in all of Europe.

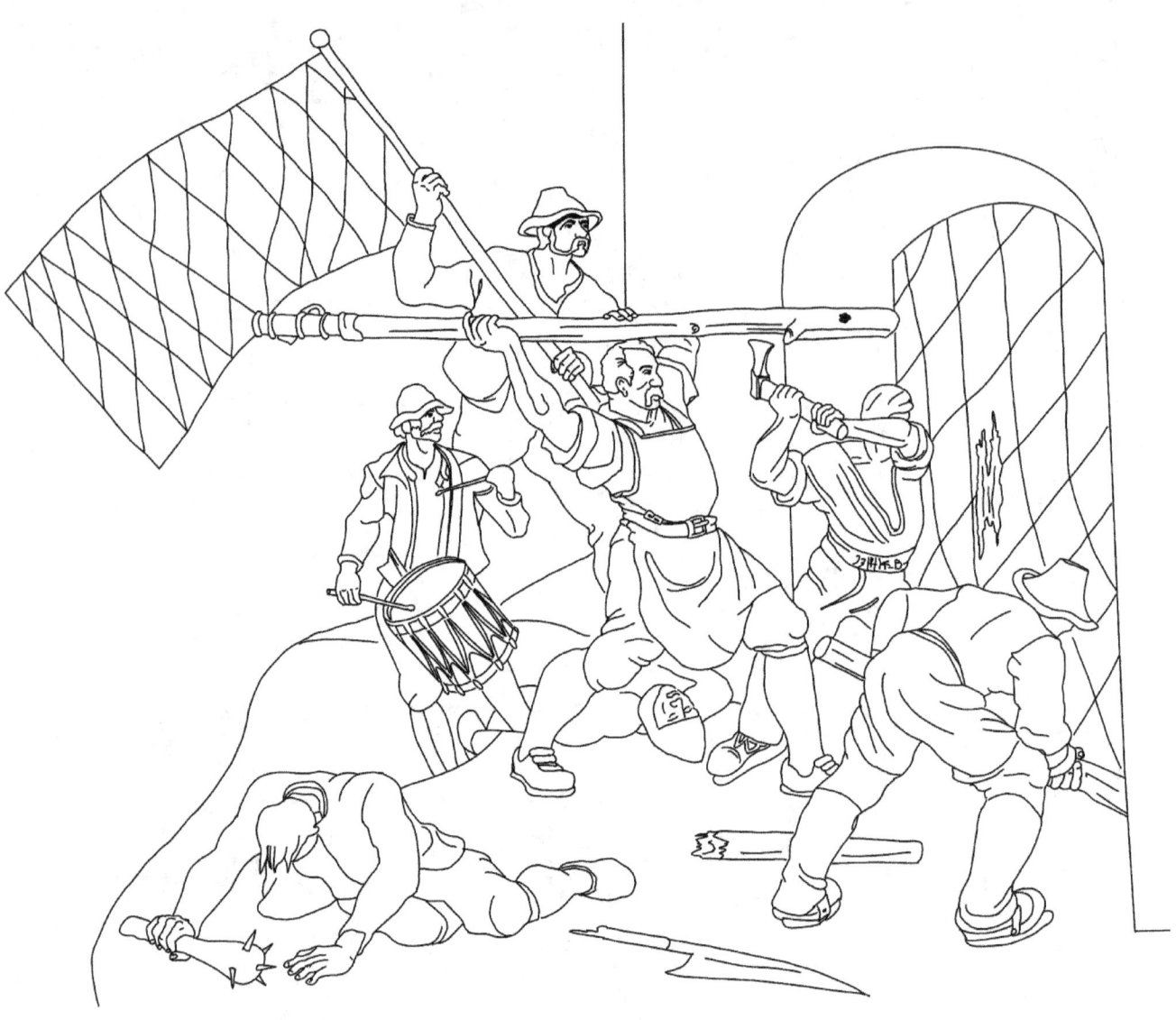

Marienplatz 5, painted by Heinrich Bickel in 1933

This Lüftlmalerei is a reproduction of another painting, "The Storming of the Red Tower in Munich by the Blacksmith from Kochel on Christmas Morning in the Year 1705" ("Erstürmung des Roten Turmes zu München durch den Schmied von Kochel am Weihnachtsmorgen des Jahres 1705"), originally painted by Franz von Defregger in 1881.

In 1705, during the War of the Spanish Succession, while Bavaria was occupied by Austrian troops, the Hapsburg Empire imposed a new set of taxes, to which the Bavarian people rebelled. The rebellion spread from the small towns to the Bavarian capital of Munich. On the night of December 25, Austrian Hapsburg soldiers confronted the rebels near Sendling, a borough of Munich. The battle is now known as the Sendling Christmas Day Massacre ("Sendlinger Mordweihnacht" in German), as an estimated 1,000 Bavarians were killed.

That particular battle became a legend in Bavaria. And no hero of the rebellion was more legendary than the Blacksmith from Kochel. More than 70 years old and standing more than 2 meters (7 feet) tall, he supposedly fought in the revolt that Christmas night carrying a 50 kg (110 lbs.) spike-studded club in one hand and the Bavarian flag in the other.

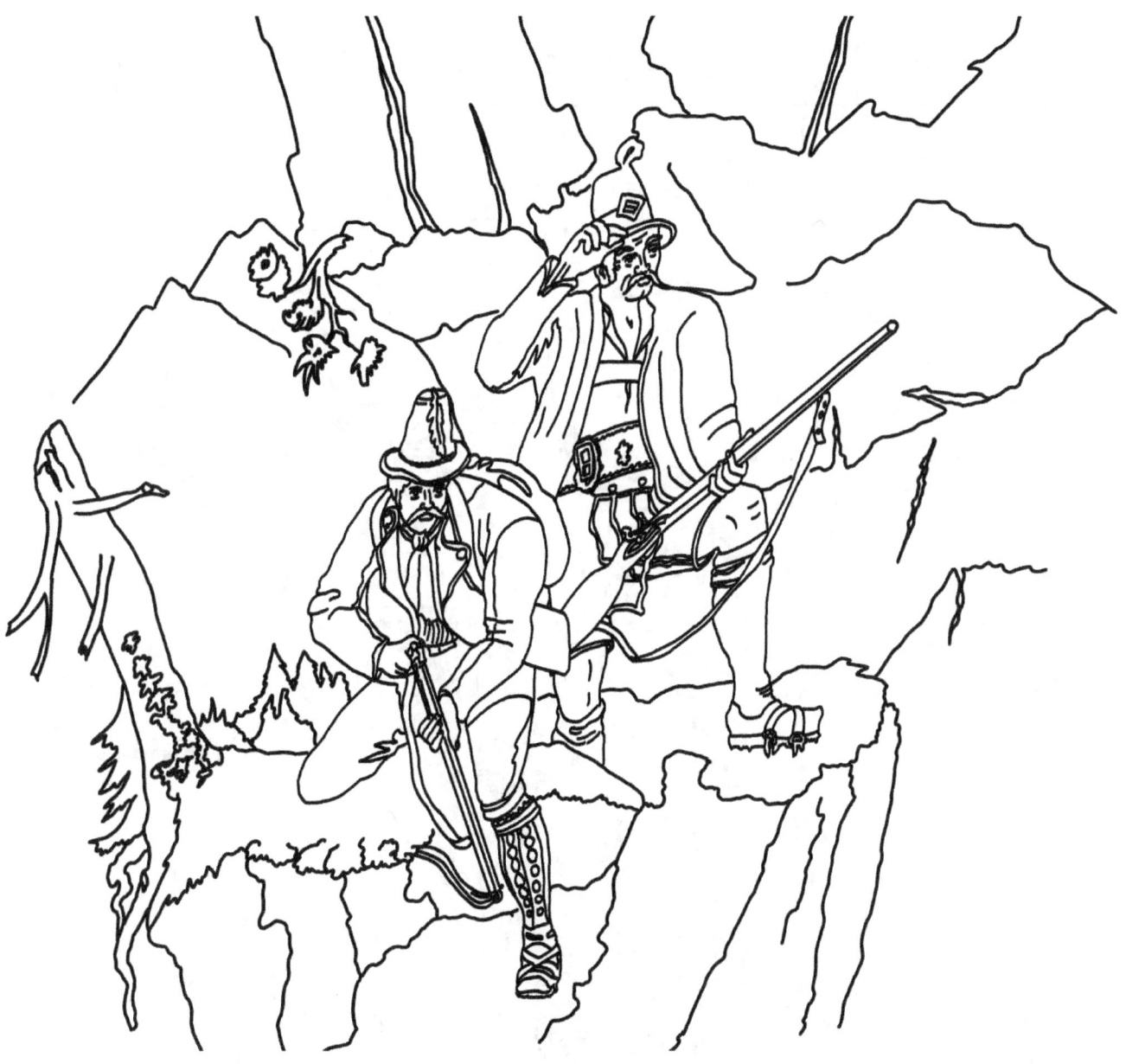

Isi's Goldener Engel, Bankgasse 5, painted by Isidor and Franz Winterholler around 1939

In 1939, Isidor Winterholler, a painter from Unterwindach, acquired this building and established an inn on the first floor, giving the house its name, Isi's Goldener Engel (or "Isi's Golden Angel").

Above the front door, a Lüftlmalerei of two Bavarian hunters in the mountains.

Atlas Post Hotel, Marienplatz 12, painted by Franz Seraph Zwinck in 1778, lost in 1889

While there are no Lüftlmalerei on the gable of the building here today, in 1778, the front of the hotel had been painted by "The Lüftlmaler from Oberammergau," Franz Seraph Zwinck (1747-1792). Zwinck's original Lüftlmalerei depicted the building of the second temple in Jerusalem, with the cedars of Lebanon being brought to the construction site by raftsmen in traditional Bavarian costumes. However, that mural fell victim to an expansion in 1889. In 1927, Professor Carl Reiser faithfully recreated the original mural that had been painted on the walls of the hotel here on the newly built building at Rathausplatz 13. Today, rather than a mural, statues representing Saints, angels, and famous people from Bavarian history adorn the walls outside the Atlas Post Hotel.

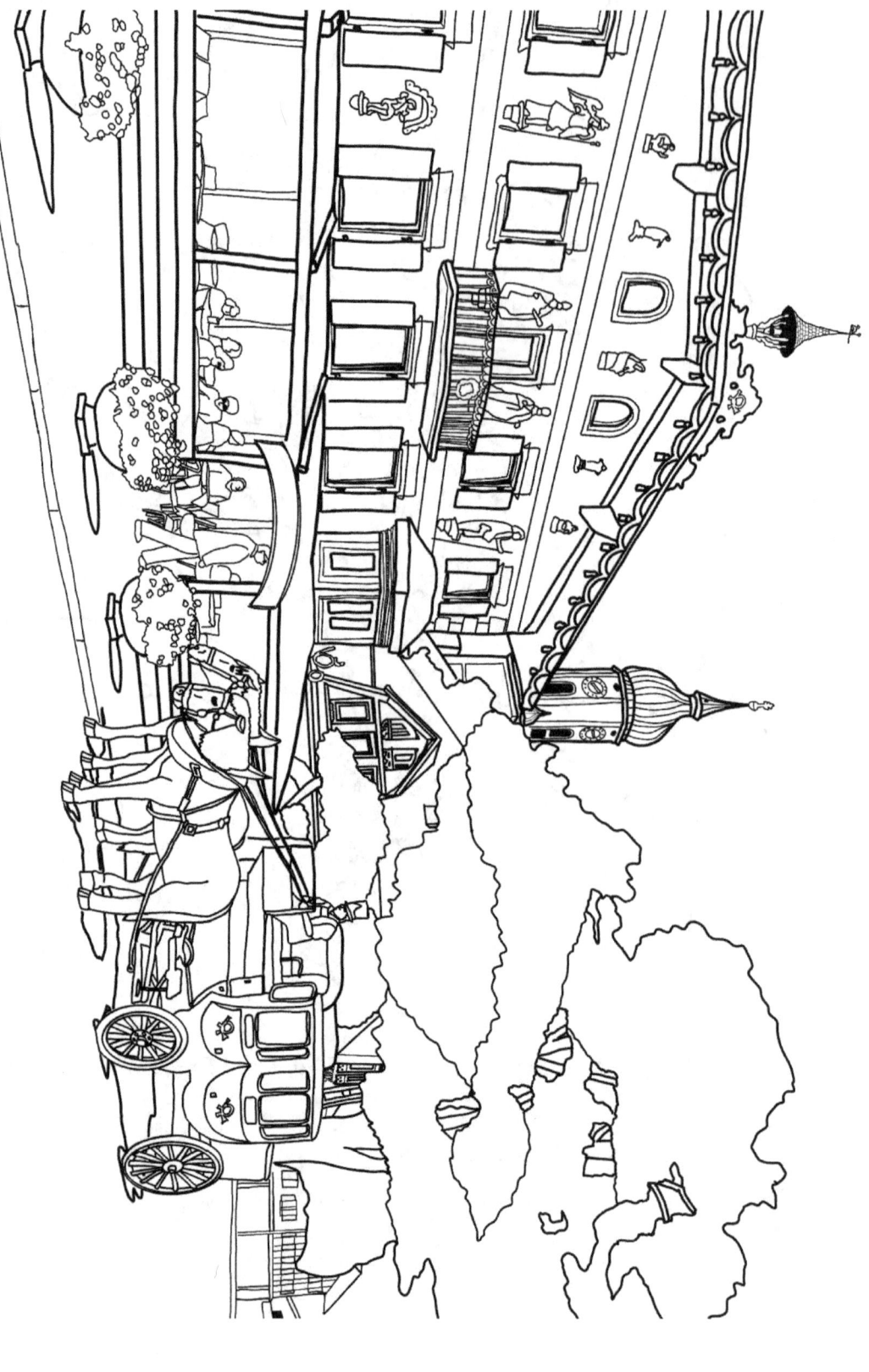

ABOUT THE BOOK

The author is a lapsed lawyer turned folk-art historian and writer living in Bavaria. Before moving to the foothills of the Alps, he had a very square job in one of those very square states out West: he was a prosecutor in Colorado. Justin Vazquez has attempted to follow in the footsteps of Franz Joseph Bronner, who, 100 years earlier, armed with a camera and a notebook, set out to catalogue every Lüftlmalerei in the area around Garmisch-Partenkirchen.

While new Lüftlmalerei may have been painted since, nothing else has changed since 1908, when Bronner wrote in *Von Deutscher Sitt' und Art*: "What summer visitor or tourist would not have enjoyed the old, gracefully painted farmhouses, of which there are still a considerable number in our high mountains! […] If one of the foreigners were to satisfy his thirst for knowledge and inquire about the creators of these paintings, he would most likely not receive half a dozen correct answers per hundred questions. Most of the locals know little or nothing about the matter, and looking up chronicles or guides does not make you feel much better. Admittedly, this painting is an art that stands in the street, and in some respects resembles folk song; one delights in these creations – without much asking who conceived them, who made them, or who brought them first."